LEGENDS OF LIGHT

LEGENDS

OF LIGHT
A Michigan Lighthouse Portfolio

Photographs by Ed Wargin

Ann Arbor Media Group

Copyright © 2005 Ed Wargin

All rights reserved. No part of this book may be reproduced in
any manner without the express written consent of the publisher,
except in the case of brief excerpts in critical reviews or articles.

All inquiries should be addressed to:
Ann Arbor Media Group LLC
2500 South State Street
Ann Arbor, MI 48104

Designed by Savitski Design, Ann Arbor, Michigan.
Printed and bound in Canada.

09 08 07 06 05   1 2 3 4 5

Library of Congress Cataloging in Publication data on file.
ISBN-13: 978-1-58726-251-7
ISBN-10: 1-58726-251-7

MEMORIAM

In memory of fellow photographer—Mr. Tim Slattery

DEDICATION

To my most favorite *Lights* in all of Michigan—Kathy-jo and Jake

Introduction

Introduction

LIKE MANY PEOPLE IN THE GREAT LAKES REGION,

I have great passion for Great Lakes heritage and culture. To me, nothing exemplifies this heritage and culture better than our Michigan lighthouses. These structures stand upon rocky islands, perch over sand dunes and forests, ride along the edges of underwater escarpments, and are quietly placed in the midst of our busiest waterways.

The idea of working on this project was thrilling; its mere scale would mean traveling *thousands of miles through our Great Lakes*. The short time frame combined with no control over the weather would make for the most interesting scenarios. More exciting, however, was the challenge of knowing that in most cases, I would have only one shot at getting the image. Many of the lights are difficult at best to reach, a situation that does not allow for mistakes. So for better or worse, lucky or unlucky, my endeavor was to show the reality of the day, pleased in the knowing that our lightkeepers experienced every conceivable weather pattern in these places, and therefore I would too.

That said, this book is not about *every* lighthouse in Michigan but, rather, is a beautiful selection of the many different *types* of lighthouses that dot our shorelines, islands, and rivers. The photographs in this book are not meant to imply that one lighthouse is better than any other. I have simply chosen the houses that I thought would best tell the story, the Legends of Light.

Granite Island Lighthouse, Lake Superior

Night had come, and it was time to rest my head. Stationed on a mass of granite outcropping in the heart of Lake Superior, I was approximately six miles north of Marquette, Michigan. I had been eagerly anticipating this duty for nearly three months, and if it weren't for the lighthouse keeper's kind invitation, I wouldn't be here. Weary from travel, I step into the assistant lightkeeper's room and close my eyes. Tomorrow was on the approach, and I must be ready to rise before the sun, prepared for another day's work.

There is no alarm to wake me, but the sound of herring gulls is a fine substitute. I dress quickly and gather my tools, trying not to wake the lighthouse keeper or his wife. Hot coffee poured, I open the Granite Island Lighthouse journal to acquaint myself with passages written not so long ago.

It is early in the month of October 1903, and the lighthouse keeper had written endlessly of mundane chores and tireless duties he performed. Most entries seem mechanical in nature, until I arrive at an entry that states:

"At 8 am John D. McMartin [the assistant lighthouse keeper] *went to boathouse, got boat and started to take it around south side of island by derrick. Keeper was going to Marquette, fresh wind from N.E. sea caught boat, smashed it against point of rocks, boat smashed to pieces, John D. McMartin was drowned—nothing was seen of body.*"

I am here because I need to know these things. I pause before I read more, not knowing what I'll find. But the next day's entry is of more chores, more duties, written by the keeper as if nothing significant happened the day before. And so I learn. If the lake didn't try to kill them, the boredom and isolation certainly would.

My reading finished, I notice that stars are still present but quickly fading. One narrow band of magenta marks the horizon miles away over the water. I must move now. With lantern in hand, I quickly move down the latticework of boulders that comprises this island, never forgetting that I am on an island that sits in a lake often known as "the meanest lake in all of North America."

I find my spot and set up my tools. I wait a bit longer for the first hint of sunlight to appear on the lighthouse, which is now incredibly high above my head. This morning, the herring gulls have many remarks for me. They are either disappointed that I have nothing for them to eat or angry that I have taken their best perching position. Whatever the case, they aren't happy with me, nor am I with them. I don't want their racket to wake the keeper before I finish my chores this first day on the island. And so I begin my work.

The arms of the sun stretch through the morning sky—CLICK. The camera speaks and I begin to capture what I came here for—CLICK—my heart rate quickens as the sun and sky work their magic, thrilling me to the bones. I imagine all the sunrises and sunsets that the keeper has seen over the years. I imagine the fear felt by the assistant lighthouse keeper as he struggled for his life on that October day, and I shudder to know that his fate was sealed on the rocky cliffs just below me now. CLICK.

Introduction

T HE SKY WAS BLUE, the water emerald green, and it seemed a perfect day. Several gulls made noise above me, and I thought for sure they were applauding my technique. It didn't take long before I realized they were laughing.

I'm finished, smiling as I sprint up toward the lighthouse. I find more coffee brewing, and the lighthouse keeper and his wife awake and moving about. A little while later, as we push off from the dock, I look back at Granite Island and the Granite Island Lighthouse. I am comforted in knowing this place, and grateful to befriend these keepers of the light, Scott and Martine Holman.

I reflect upon my stay and what it felt like pretending to be a lighthouse keeper for a day. I realize it's a life none of us may ever experience again. Yet through the efforts of preservation, many of us will be allowed to walk imaginary footsteps in those cherished places of history.

I am not a lighthouse keeper. I am not a painter. I am not a writer. I am a photographer, and I am grateful for the chance to tell stories through my camera.

Waugoshance Lighthouse, Lake Michigan, Part I

It's early morning and I set out from the western edge of Wilderness State Park. Lake Michigan is calm and I had been anticipating this kayak trip to Waugoshance Lighthouse for quite some time. I thought I would paddle directly up to the lighthouse, affording me the best opportunity to photograph this aging pillar in the water.

I have paddled enough to know that I should always travel with a paddling buddy, but summer in northern Michigan is a busy time for my friends. So rather than wait for a gap in someone else's schedule, I decided to strike out on my own. The paddling was easy and the water warm as it dripped off my paddle and onto my hands. I could easily see the bottom of the lake as well as the point of land named Waugoshance as it lay before me to the north and west.

The sky was blue, the water emerald green, and it seemed a perfect day. Several gulls made noise above me, and I thought for sure they were applauding my technique. It didn't take long before I realized they were laughing.

After much paddling, I begin to see the lighthouse on the not-so-distant horizon. I am lost in the thrill of my successful plan when all of sudden I am introduced to Mother Nature's dearest friend, Mr. Wind. Now, Mr. Wind seemed particularly urgent in his manner to go somewhere right then and I was in his way. He was much stronger than the Mr. Wind the weather service spoke of the night before, and I was awash in waves. The gulls, however, were enjoying their belly laughs from the safety of the air above me.

And then, in what seemed a single stroke of my paddle, the waves jumped from one foot to four feet high, rolling past me with great velocity. I quickly realized that I would not be photographing the lighthouse today but, rather, surviving my trip out to the lighthouse instead. It was my own darn fault. I knew not to paddle alone. As often happens I was possessed by a project, and in my search for a different perspective had convinced myself that paddling up to the lighthouse solo was the only way to achieve it.

Yielding to the wind, I turn my kayak around and head back to safe harbor. I look back at the lighthouse and know I wouldn't reach her, at least not today. And so my strokes took on new meaning and the gulls stopped laughing. They merely watched as my little red and white kayak cut into the waves like an old daredevil lure being pulled along the surface of the waves.

All the while, as I try to paddle my way to safety, I rationalize all the things I will do better if I get back to land. I will take out the garbage without grumbling. I will go to the grocery store with an actual smile on my face. I will learn how to fold a towel with the stripe on the inside. It is then as I find myself in the midst of this bargaining that the irony of the situation overwhelms me. I am working on a project about lighthouses, laced with stories of shipwrecks and missing boaters, rescue missions and safe passages.

I am renewed. These lighthouses are important for us to know about. Unfortunately, Mr. Wind feels I should visit this lighthouse some other day. And I will.

Detroit River Lighthouse, Lake Erie

Many years ago, my wife and I lived out west, where I worked as a commercial photographer. As a young man gaining photo experience, I had the fortuitous opportunity to work with our nation's finest car photographers, most of them from Detroit, Michigan. Every spring they arrived to photograph new prototypes in the desert, and I would assist them, lugging heavy photo equipment and finding the best locations for them. My wife and I are originally from northern Minnesota, so at that time, as a transplant to the west, I felt compelled to tell these fellow northerners false stories about killer snakes and jumping spiders. Nonetheless, we all got along quite well, and they eventually forgave me for the stories. In kind, they introduced me to the automotive advertising industry, and in return, I eventually forgave them for that.

One such friend from those days still lives and works in the Motor City. I asked if he knew of anyone who could take me to the Detroit River Lighthouse. As fate would have it, he fancied himself a boat captain and proclaimed to me the worthiness of his boat. It was a date.

I live several hours north of Detroit, where I begin my drive packed to the gills with gear. Without fanfare, woods turn into silver buildings, and glimmering lakes turn into shallow malls. I weave my way to the studio where I meet my friend and we drive east twenty minutes to the marina. It is autumn now and the winds are chilly. This, he says, will be the last trip for the boat this season. I am honored.

I load my gear into the boat and am informed that we will have additional guests for the ride. They arrive, and it is visually apparent that I am the only one from the north. The guests are pleasant, well groomed, and good-looking, and I, suddenly, am feeling a bit rough around the edges. Nonetheless, the boat peels back from the slip and we head toward open water.

We are north of Grosse Pointe, Michigan, and gliding past some of the wealthiest neighborhoods in our nation, where mansions stack up one after the other like cordwood. Moments later, we are slipping by some of the poorest. These images hurt my head, as the visual discrepancy doesn't make sense. Soon, emerging from the shadows are the world headquarters for General Motors Corporation and downtown Detroit, where an amazing broad stalk of glass and metal rises, gently sweeping back again into a sea of warehouses and businesses which turn into gray smokestacks and factories, most likely churning out steel. We slip under the Ambassador Bridge, which connects the United States to Canada. It's full of trucks prepared to cross their commerce over the international border. As I note this, I wrestle with my purpose and almost forget why I'm here. But then I see my camera bag on the floor and remember that I am here for the lighthouse.

Faster now, as the sun starts to fall, we cut a deeper track into the water and pull closer to the lighthouse. Positioned in the middle of the waterway, it's the only thing around for miles. I am a little concerned about the sky as there are no clouds, just pale blue light. I stare at the lighthouse and wonder how I am going to create a nice picture. Behind me, the sun seems intent on dropping like a piece of molten steel made from the factory we saw earlier in the day.

My palms start to sweat as I hope I haven't made my friend take me on this journey—this one shot, one last boat ride of the season opportunity—for nothing. The crew is alive now and goading me into setting up so they can watch me work. The captain, my old friend and fellow photographer, is perfect to be with today. He treats the lighthouse as if it was a car and quietly—without us speaking to each other—positions the boat as if he were setting up his own gear to shoot a car. He gives me a straight on view. A three-quarter front view. A backlit view. He is an expert and gives me more views than I hope for. At this moment he is actually inside my brain, communicating with a certain photo-speak engaged by nods and expression, flawlessly following my silent gestures for different angles.

I worry, however, that I may not be getting a unique shot. As I converse with my own self-talk, the crew turns into something truly horrific to any former commercial photographer. They become art directors. Behind me I hear voices dispersing advice on angle, composition, and technique, and I freeze. Don't make eye contact. The sun tips below the horizon and the sweet light is happening "now." The captain, still reading my cues, stealthily backs the boat closer to the light and, when I peek back at him, senses my desperation. I look into the viewfinder and that's when it happened. A lone gull pulls a beautiful 360 degrees around the top of the lighthouse, allowing me one click as the sun radiates off of his white belly. I have my shot. As the self-appointed art directors talk about how they would have taken the shot, I look back at the captain, my trusted friend, and give him a nod. We are done.

As I finish, the seamless nature of life becomes apparent. As I mentioned earlier, I met the captain, my photographer friend, more than ten years ago while photographing autos in the west. Who ever could have guessed all those years ago, as we stood in a desert as young men with promise, that we would one day be on the Detroit River together shooting the lighthouse that protected the ships that moved the steel that made the cars. It all makes sense. Life is a great wheel on an axle. It all goes round and round, making perfect sense, and today I am convinced that it is the lighthouse that brings us both together to realize how small—and intertwined—the world really is.

Legends of Light

LIKE A VACUUM, the wind pulls the door beneath the wing. And there it is, Waugoshance Lighthouse…that's when the magic happened. I was no longer a photographer with a pilot, I was his tail gunner and we were going to strafe this lighthouse with seven frames of film per second.

Waugoshance Lighthouse

Waugoshance Lighthouse, Lake Michigan, Part II

Having failed my first attempt to reach Waugoshance Lighthouse, I enlist the help of a dear friend and his motorboat. I deem him a most seaworthy captain and a perfect partner-in-crime for the elusive Waugoshance. We'll make it, I know we will. Nothing scares this friend. An emergency room physician, he has a brave demeanor that draws deep respect from me in all ways. His exploits in the outdoors have become legendary stories of success in our household, and I know today will be no different. We launch from Mackinaw City Marina and quickly head north and west toward the Mackinac Bridge.

The bridge comes into view as we pass through the marina pier. The water is calm, as it was on my first effort. The weather report indicates a small chop today, but his 23-foot boat is capable, and we quickly cruise through the Straits of Mackinac without incident. But the calm is short-lived. The chop gave way to white caps; the white caps gave way to waves in the 5-foot range. The waves continue to grow, but clearly we see Waugoshance, only one mile away from of us now. I know we'll make it this time.

But here's the math. The boat cut a 3-foot draft; we were in approximately 5 feet of rolling waves; and the depth of the lake in this location is 11 feet on a calm day. Clearly, it doesn't add up. With every pitch we see the bottom of the lake as clearly as we see our own feet. But yet, I'm thinking, well, if he's not saying anything…I'm not saying anything. And that's when it happened. The captain of steel in a calm voice, but with eyes as big as dinner plates, announced that our fate may be in peril and we should head back immediately. I wanted to say I agree, but my heart was lodged in my throat and I couldn't make a noise. I just nodded my head in agreement and accepted that Waugoshance had sent me home once again.

Beaver Island Light, Lake Michigan

This project has made the importance of lighthouses very clear to me. They have saved untold lives, made sure the goods we rely on reach their destinations, and provided safe passage for countless ships on our Great Lakes.

It's early December, and I'm excited as I drive from my home in Petoskey to Charlevoix. I steal a quick glance at Round Lake as I come into town, taking notice of how calm the water is for such a frigid winter day.

Thousands of passengers have traveled on the ferryboat *Emerald Isle* between Charlevoix and Beaver Island. The *Emerald Isle* is on one of its last trips to the island for the season, and today I board thinking the ride will be easy, even serene.

I pay and get my truck settled, then hunker down in the lobby at the Beaver Island Boat Company. As I hide behind an old issue of *Time* magazine, I hear a conversation at the front desk. The clerk is speaking to her customer, a native Beaver Islander. "The captain isn't very talkative today. The only time he is not talkative is when the water gets really rough."

I don't pay much heed and choose to keep reading. Shortly, one more customer arrives, another native islander, who is given the status of the impending ride. Immediately she phones the local airport, asks a few questions, and screams with joy. The last seat on the plane is hers, and she takes it without hesitation.

Not to worry.

The boat arrives an hour late, but nonetheless ready to take us to the island. The last bits of produce and lumber loaded, a smiling face greets me and takes my ticket. A face that almost implies, if only in my imagination,…hello sucker.

But I am not deterred. I admire the true sailors of the Great Lakes, the real heroes who've passed before me. To falter now just wouldn't seem right. As I stand on the boat bundled in high-tech waterproof clothing, windproof hat, fingerless gloves, and moisture wicking longjohns, I think of the sailors, seamen, boaters, commercial fishermen, and even passengers who have plied these waters before me wearing thick scratchy wool coats and deerskin choppers. Maybe a long knit scarf if they were lucky.

For my own comfort, I rationalize that boating today is far safer than it was 50 years ago, and a quantum leap better than it was a hundred years ago, when the best navigation tools on the lake were a lighthouse and a brave ship captain. Today, with GPS mapping devices, high-tech compasses, cellular phones, and weather radios attached to our belts, navigating the lakes has become more science than art. But it is the art that brings me on this journey.

I'm in the boat now and looking upon the placid waters of Round Lake, thinking to myself this won't be so bad. It's calm. I believe that although this boat is called a ferry, it sure looks and feels like a ship.

I sit up toward the front of the boat and settle into my seat, ready to relax. Keeping my mind off the ride, I fall into lazy sleep. But not for long. All of a sudden I hear grown men—not men in suits and penny loafers but men born with 5 o'clock shadows and hands the size of melons—crying, "Oh my God, what did we get ourselves into today!" I am awake now. The men barely finish their sentiments when a huge wave crashes over the entire front end of the boat and spreads itself like a demon on top of the windows.

I wasn't quite sure what happened during my brief nap, but who stole the ship? The ship I was on seemed so large and weighty before I began to doze, and now it's as if I'm in a 16-foot Lund, a type of fishing boat I spent the summers of my youth riding in northern Minnesota.

Boom! With ferocious intensity, another wave smashes against the boat and reels my eyes into the back of my head. I get my bearings and watch in amazement as I'm introduced to the next few hours of my life. And in this life there are only two points of view, water and sky. Punctuated by the pounding of waves, one after the other in a relentless, mean-spirited assault on the boat, I see water. And then sky. Water, and sky.

That's when it occurs to me. *This ride is perfect*. I couldn't think of a better way to experience what life may have been like on the Great Lakes. For me, much of the travel for this project has been via my truck. It's been my sleeping quarters, kitchen, office, changing room, my place out of the rain, and my own music studio. Today, while the water is cresting at nearly 12 feet high and turning burly men into frightened little boys, and while others are sick in the on-board bathrooms, I realize the captain of this boat is one great captain, belonging to a collective of other great captains. We are in good hands.

I catch a narrow glimpse between water and sky now, and see a strip of land with a lighthouse on each end. This narrow strip of heaven is Beaver Island, and it will be my home for the next few days. Between heaven and earth, there is usually light. And today's light looks worth preserving—if only on film.

Waugoshance Lighthouse, Lake Michigan, Part III

We have some dear friends in northern Michigan, and their son, an accomplished skydiver, was offering skydiving clinics for those brave enough to jump from a plane. The thought occurred to me that perhaps he could fly me over Waugoshance Lighthouse.

He was more than willing to help, as long as I paid for gas and was flexible with his flying schedule. What a nice young man. We made plans and decided to meet at a nearby airport. What he neglected to tell me, however, was that he was not the pilot. I had just assumed he was.

I was waiting for our meeting, going over last minute changes to camera gear and film and thinking about the hundreds of times that I have flown. The plane was a wingover Cessna 172, and I could shoot down toward the ground by sticking my camera nose out of a glass side window.

But the squealing tires of a sports car zooming toward me quickly broke those thoughts. A young man steps out of the car and charges toward the plane. "Are you ready to go?" he asks. "Sure," I blurt out. We approach the plane and he opens my door. Perfect for skydiving, not so much for shooting with only one seat (the pilot's seat). He points to a loose nylon seatbelt crumpled on the floor of the small plane. Nonetheless, I act confident, as if this is an everyday occurrence. I jump into the plane and settle myself on the floor. I hear the door close behind me and am now facing the rear of the plane. I look to my side and see nothing but door. The window I was planning to shoot out of is well above my head.

Shortly after, as the pilot jumps into his seat, he points to a nearby pack with long straps setting on the floor. He quickly tells me that in case something goes awry, pull my feet through each lower strap and my arms through each upper strap. "Jump away from the plane and pull this cord," he states. Then adding a final "Good luck."

I try to gather my wits as the plane is revved up and taxiing on the runway. "Awry?" I think to myself. In the countless times I've flown, I've never before had a fifteen second parachute lesson. My brain is scrambling for answers so I blurt out, "Where did you learn to fly anyway?" He snorts back, "in the United States Army." Soon we are in the air, flying high over Little Traverse Bay and Lake Michigan. It's then the pilot yells to me, "Where are we going anyway?" I am sitting backward on the floor of a plane unable to see anything, staring at the parachute I might have to use, and he wants to know where we are going.

I crank and distort and wrench my back to look toward the front of the plane and to help direct the young pilot to the lighthouse. Somehow, I manage a glimpse over the dashboard and see a speck of lighthouse just past the point of land called Waugoshance. "There," I shout, pointing in the direction of the lighthouse. Flying north, the pilot sees it and takes a bead on it.

But I am perplexed about how to reach the window. Approaching the lighthouse, the pilot informs me that I should prepare to open the door. The door? No way. He must mean the window. But he looks at me again and states that I should prepare to open the door. I reel; he can't mean the door, he must mean the window. I am bewildered. Calmly, he shows me the door handle and instructs me on how to turn it. So I do.

Like a vacuum, the wind pulls the door beneath the wing. And there it is, Waugoshance Lighthouse. I ask the pilot to swing around for a pass so I can get my bearings. We then come out of a banking turn and I see the tip of the sun beginning to rise over Lake Huron to the east.

And that's when the magic happened. I was no longer a photographer with a pilot, I was his tail gunner and we were going to strafe this lighthouse with seven frames of film per second. And that we did while the sun draped its magenta cape all around it. One pass. Two passes. Three passes and we had our mission on film. I had gotten what I came for so I pulled the door shut and headed back to base.

On our way in, I allowed myself one last chance to peer at Waugoshance through one of the small side windows. I finally fooled her the only way that I knew how. The same winds that pushed me back two times via water had now carried me gracefully over the top of her.

Thunder Bay Island Lighthouse, Lake Huron

I contacted the preservation group for Thunder Bay Island Lighthouse through their Web site. Not knowing how to get out to that island, I sent an email, and quickly a response came, with the name of someone in his or her group who might be able to help me.

I was nervous, but those nerves calmed as soon as I spoke with the person. Kind and generous, she assured me that she would help me get out to the lighthouse.

The lighthouse is stationed approximately 12 miles out from the small town of Alpena, in Lake Huron on Thunder Bay Island. The group was excited to have someone visit their lighthouse and photograph it, especially since its exterior had just received a beautiful new coat of white paint and been painstakingly restored.

I arranged the boat ride to the island and the meeting with my contact person. I met her early one morning at a marina parking lot and she informed me that she and her staff were riding a barge carrying building supplies to the island. I could ride with them, she said, or I could ride with the two gentlemen standing near the small boat stationed at the bottom of the launch.

I thought about the barge and I looked at the two gentlemen with their smaller, faster boat. Not wanting to lose out on any chance for great skies, I decided to go with the two men. We went almost effortlessly across the water, paralleling a stretch of land for several miles, no island in site. I noticed then that over my shoulder to the west, the clouds did not look gracious. They were dark and looming as if a storm were brewing. I became anxious, as my opportunity to work in good light seemed to be slipping away in short order. This was my only chance to shoot this lighthouse, and now I was obviously going to be competing with the weather.

So as it goes, I had done a lot of assuming. I thought the lighthouse would be near the dock, but approaching the island I saw that the dock was on the west side, the lighthouse was on the east. The captain, who didn't seem to appreciate my quest for shooting in great light as much as I did, decided to show the other guest on the boat an underwater shipwreck near the south end of the island before getting us to the dock. Now don't get me wrong, the captain is a great guy and, like most folks of his age, has learned to smell the roses. I, on the other hand, was dealing with the thorns. We pulled over the top of a boiler that lay on the bottom of the shoals. It made my heart skip a beat but reminded me, once again, of the important role these lighthouses and life saving stations have played in so many lives.

Eventually, we reach the dock; I gather my 45 pounds of gear, sling it on my back, and ask, "How far is it?" "About a half-mile or so," answers the captain. Looking toward the sky, I realize my window of sun will last only another ten minutes or so and foolishly convince myself that I can do this. I look down at my hiking boots and I start running. I was striding along, okay, thundering along the trail as fast I could go. Finally, I hit an open grassy area near the lighthouse, but the sun was gone.

Muscles aching, heart pounding, I gather myself. I head toward the shoreline, scurrying past the lighthouse and through brambles to the limestone-laden shoreline. I feel defeated, and did not know how to resurrect a beautiful photograph in the now predominantly gray light. Stormy skies looming, I walk close to the waters edge where I find countless pools of water bowled up inside the limestone shore. And there it was, an opportunity as only nature can provide. Everywhere I look, small pools are reflecting the dark skies and I know at once that I should lie down on my stomach and shoot to capture the reflection of that freshly painted white lighthouse inside these pools of water. There, I thought. I have my shot. Well almost.

I lay quietly concentrating on my compositions, exposures, shutter speeds and f/stops, lost inside photography and art, making pictures once again by the narrowest of margins. And only then, as I peak inside my camera's viewfinder, do I see them. Two sets of arms waving back and forth at me. Waving hello. My two companions from the boat had made quick time to the lighthouse and made their way to the top of the light, and like two crows on the top of a pine tree, were waving their wings to say hello.

And so I do what anyone else would do in my position. I wave back. I'm no fool. These fellows are my ride off the island. I wait patiently, and tell myself that maybe I need to stop and smell the roses too. Soon enough, they made their way inward, and I made the shot I was so excited to make moments earlier.

Back at the lighthouse, I was invited to inspect the interior, and I promptly accept the offer. The rooms were intact, empty. Still painted in the original colors, I imagine who may have lived and worked here over those many years that this lighthouse was in service. What did the keepers see? Did they have children? What did they eat? What games did they play?

Lost inside each room and photographing intently, I feel ghostly memories all around me. Stepping out and sitting down with all of the volunteers as we ate lunch, I listen to the stories of pride they feel about preserving this lighthouse. And then, I too begin to feel pride in what I am doing, knowing that images of these lighthouses are a form of preservation too. I guess we all have our ways of contributing.

It is here that I finally learn what is most important to take away from this project. Think for a moment with me, if you will about the premise of a lighthouse. They were built to create safe passage for goods and materials, but most important, to help save the lives of men and women. Today, with perfect irony, the lighthouses are being saved in return.

Conclusion

I hope this book will encourage people to pay heed to these inspiring icons of our Great Lakes. Each time you pay a fee to see a lighthouse, remember you are helping to preserve that lighthouse, and that is something of which to be proud.

As well, take time to visit your local library or bookstore and learn more about our Great Lakes heritage. You can also go on-line and visit many wonderful Web sites dedicated to many of the lighthouses in this book. Consider becoming a member of their organizations. Your support will help keep these lighthouses alive and in good order. Remember, nothing speaks more of our heritage than these beacons, and it is up to all of us to keep our lighthouses safe from ruin.

For the more adventurous, consider becoming a lighthouse keeper through the many programs that allow individuals or couples to participate by living at a lighthouse while volunteering as the guest keeper and caretaker. But most of all, please visit, enjoy, and respect our beautiful Legends of Light.

Legends of Light

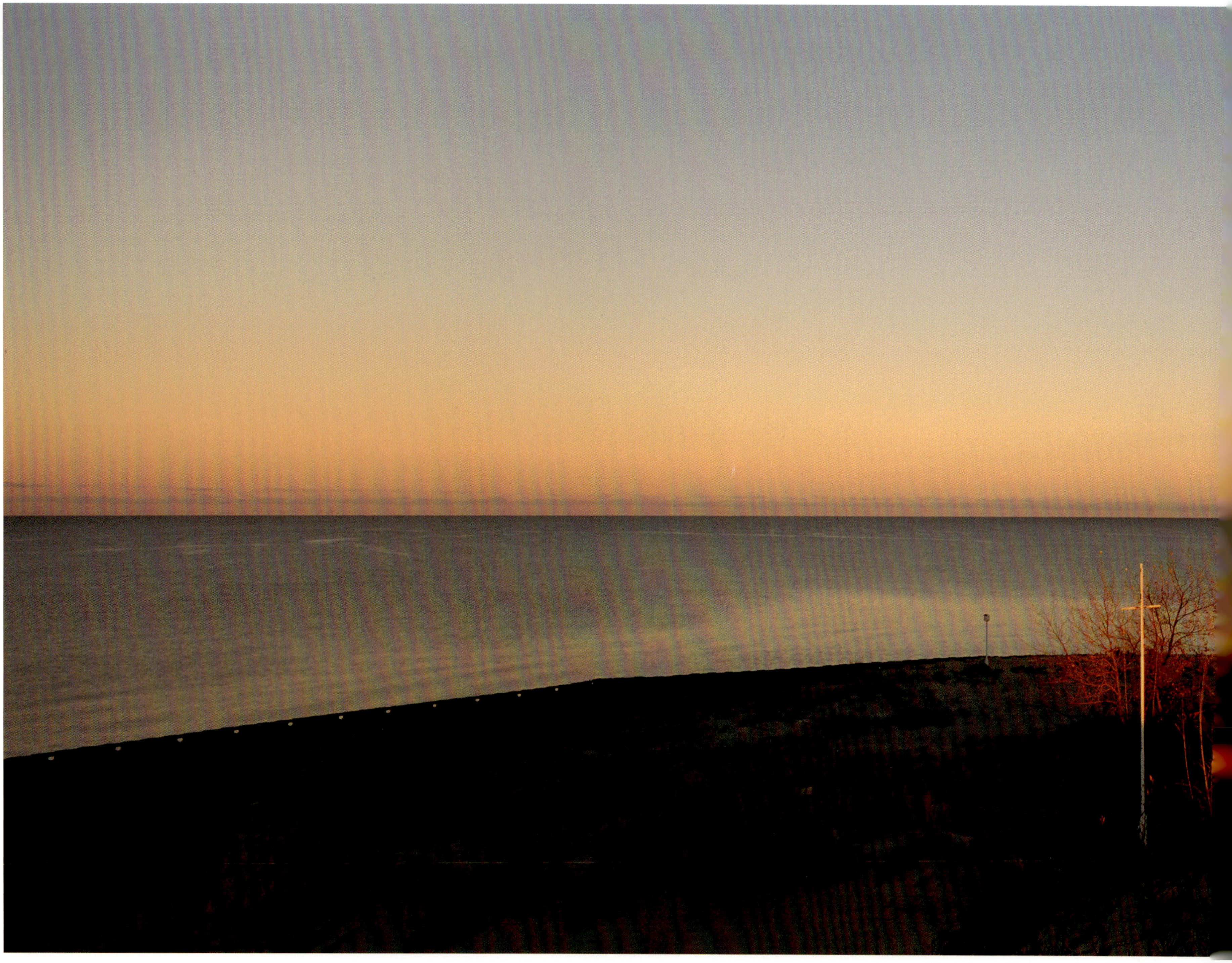

BIG SABLE POINT ▲ *Est. 1867 Lake Michigan*

CRISP POINT ▲ *Est. 1904 Lake Superior*

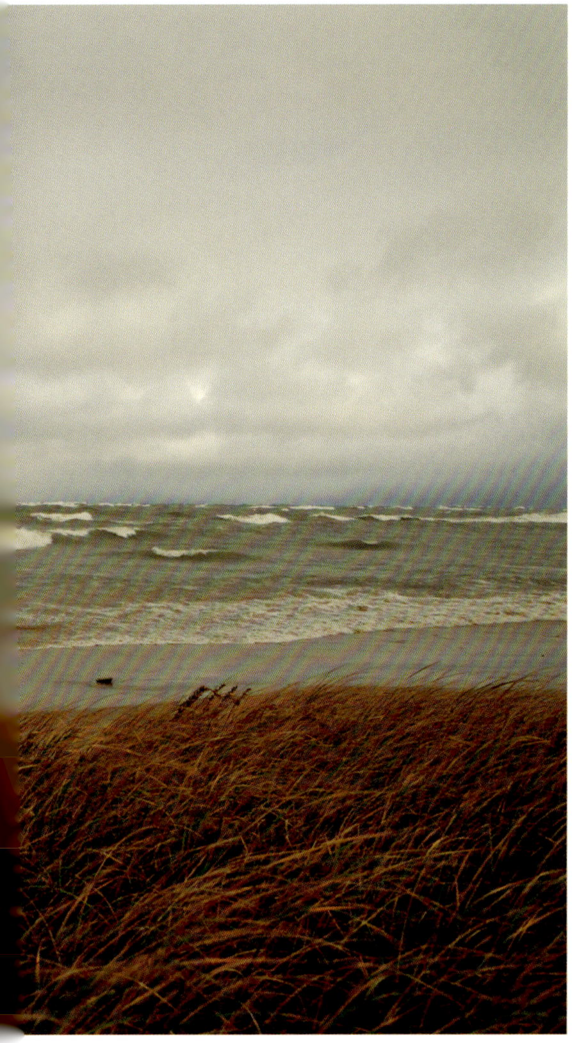

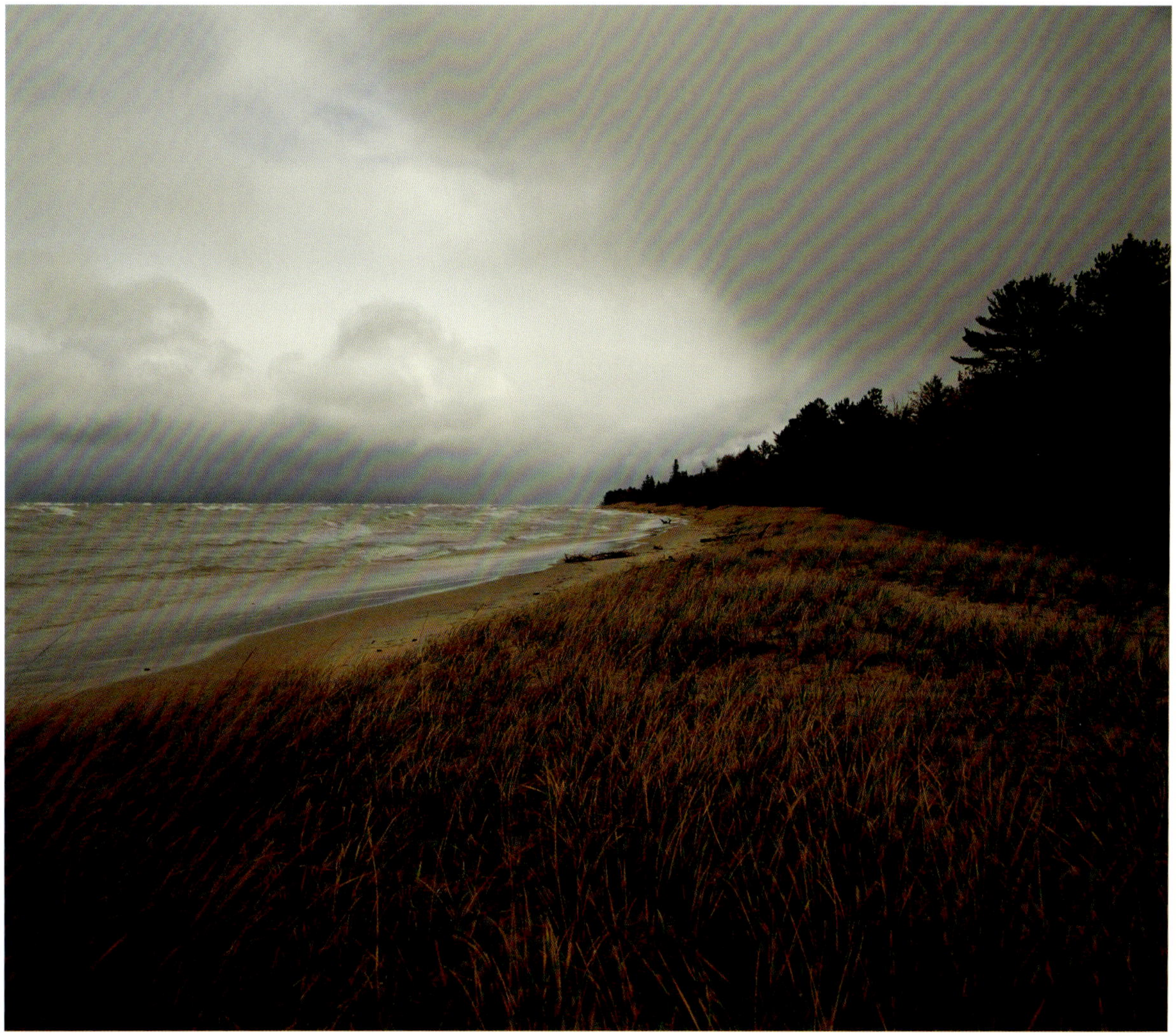

GRANITE ISLAND ⚓ *Est. 1868 Lake Superior*

New Presque Isle ▲ Est. 1870 Lake Huron

GRANITE ISLAND   *Est. 1868 Lake Superior*

THE SHIPWRECK *BERMUDA*   *Murray Bay, Lake Superior*

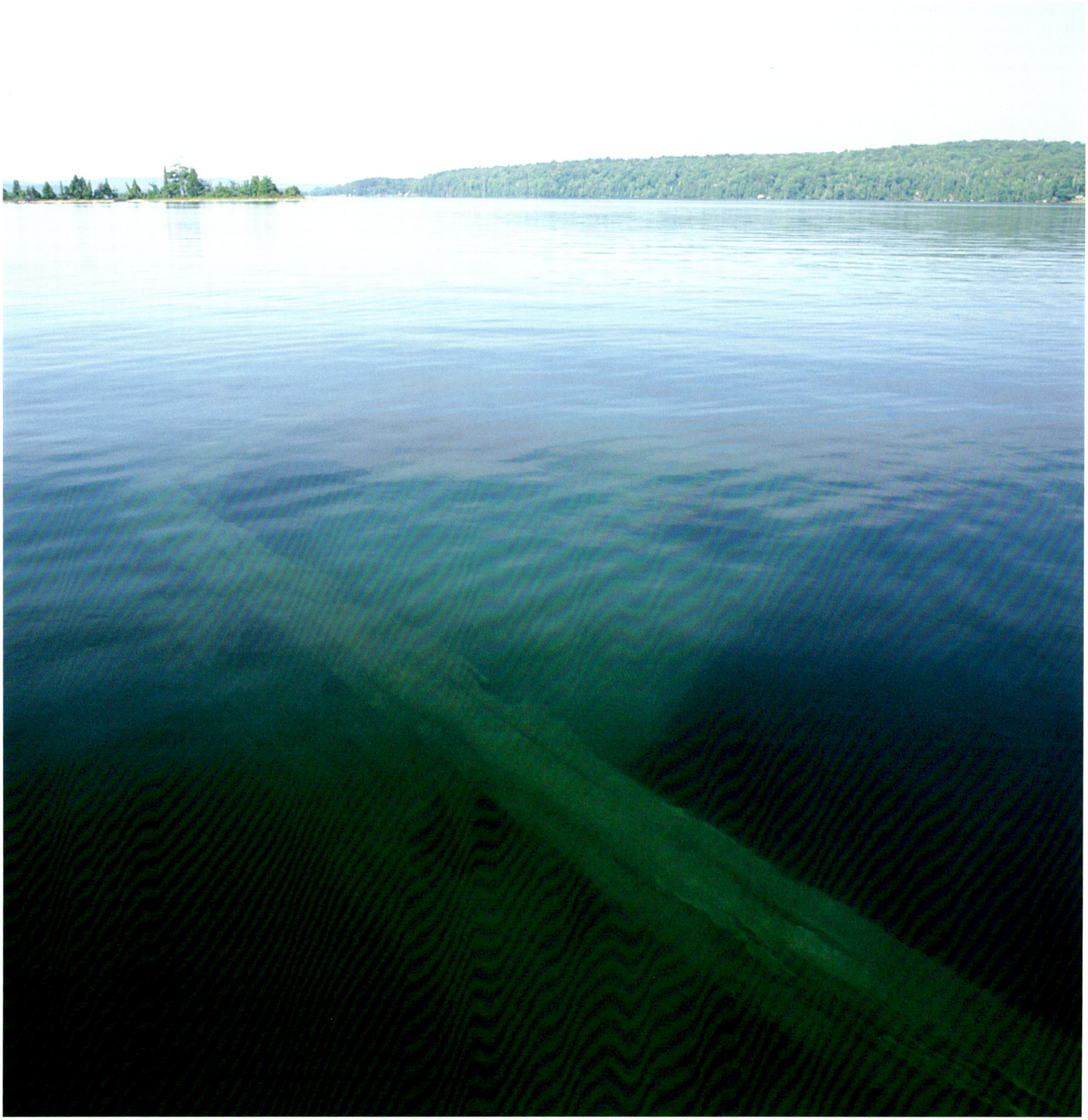

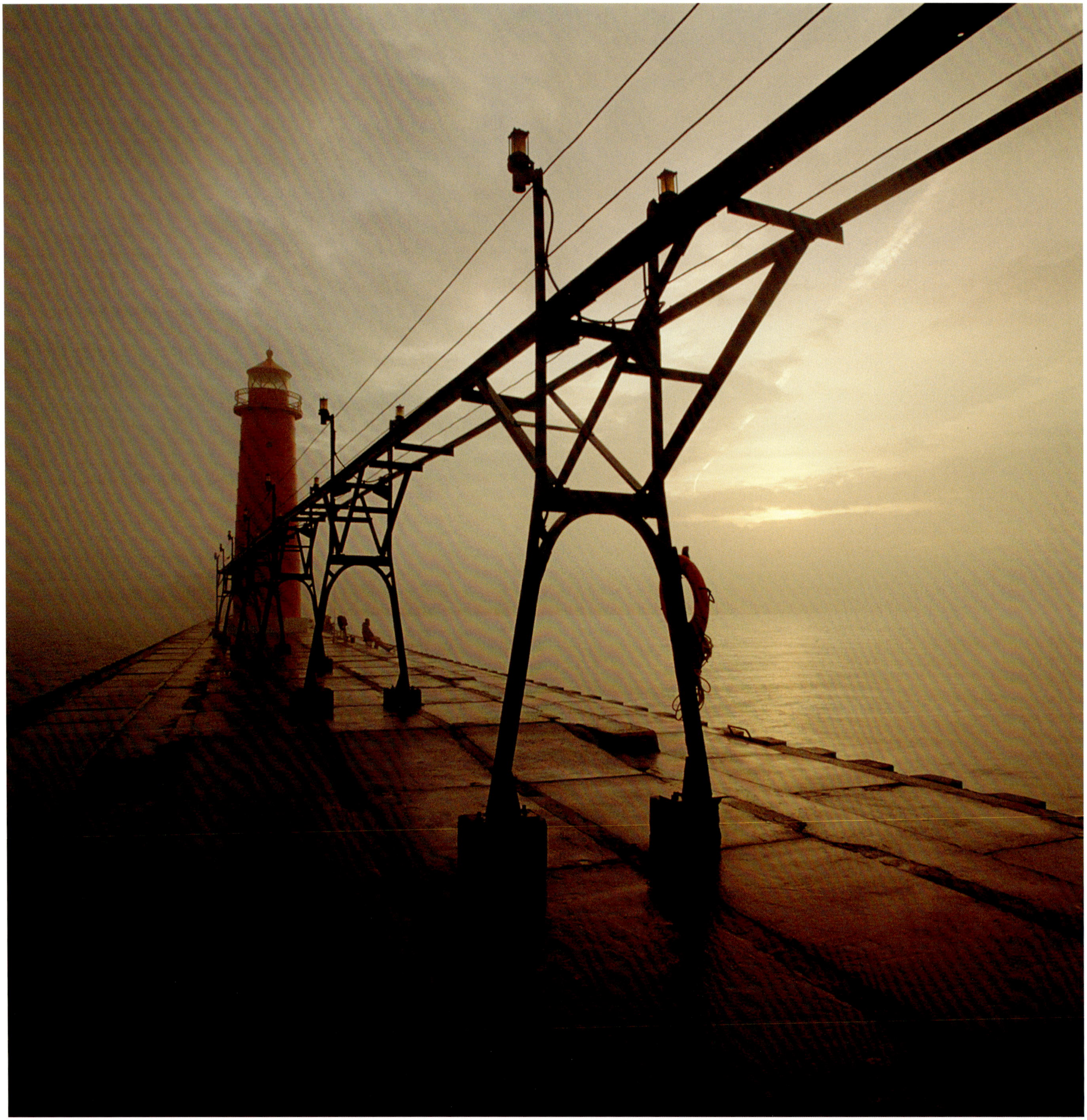

Wreckage on the Beach ◢ *Beaver Island, Lake Michigan*

Grand Haven ◂ *Est. 1839 Lake Michigan*

PETOSKEY PIERHEAD ▲ Est. 1899 Lake Michigan

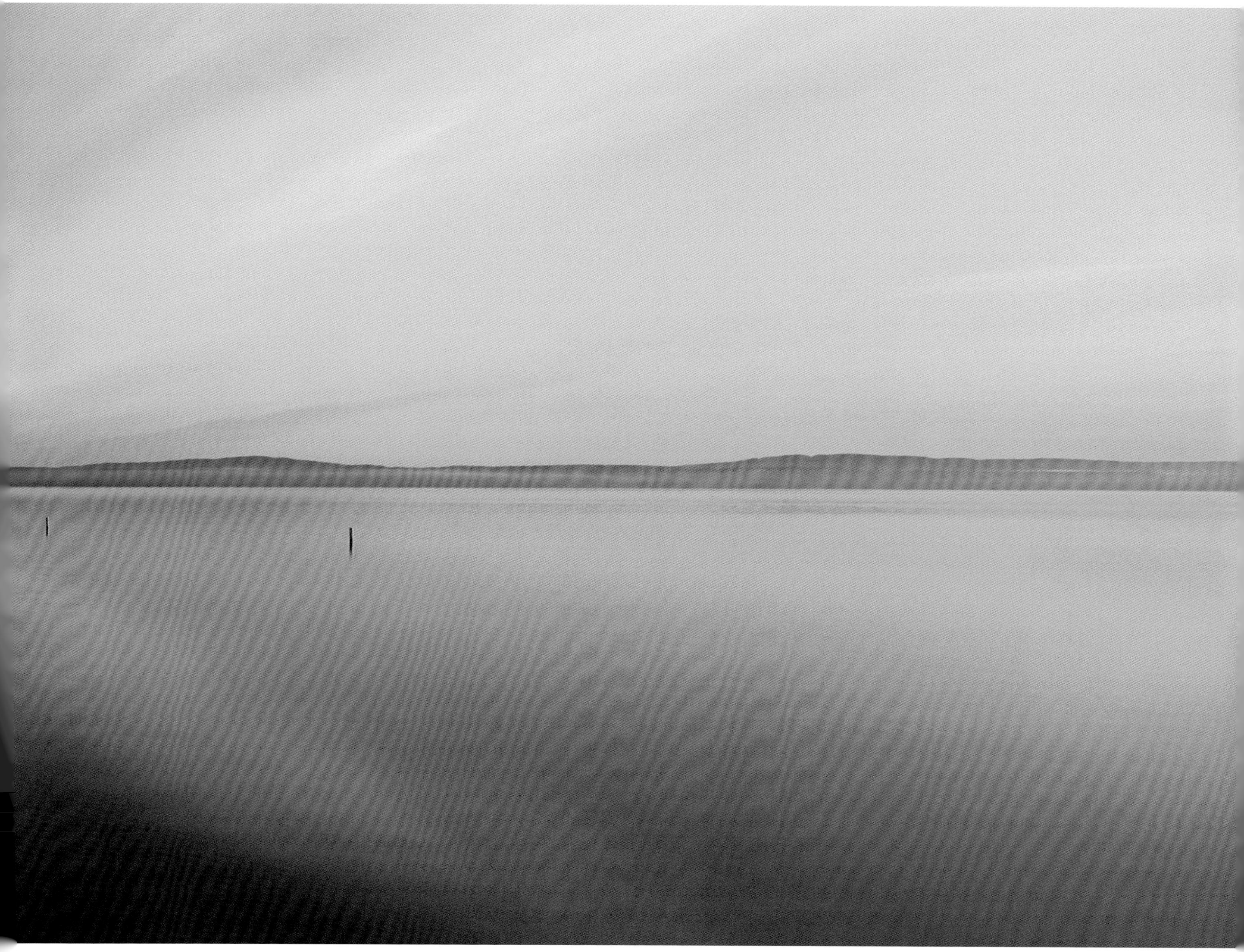

POINT IROQUOIS △ *Est. 1855 Lake Superior*

STURGEON POINT ▷ *Est. 1870 Lake Huron*

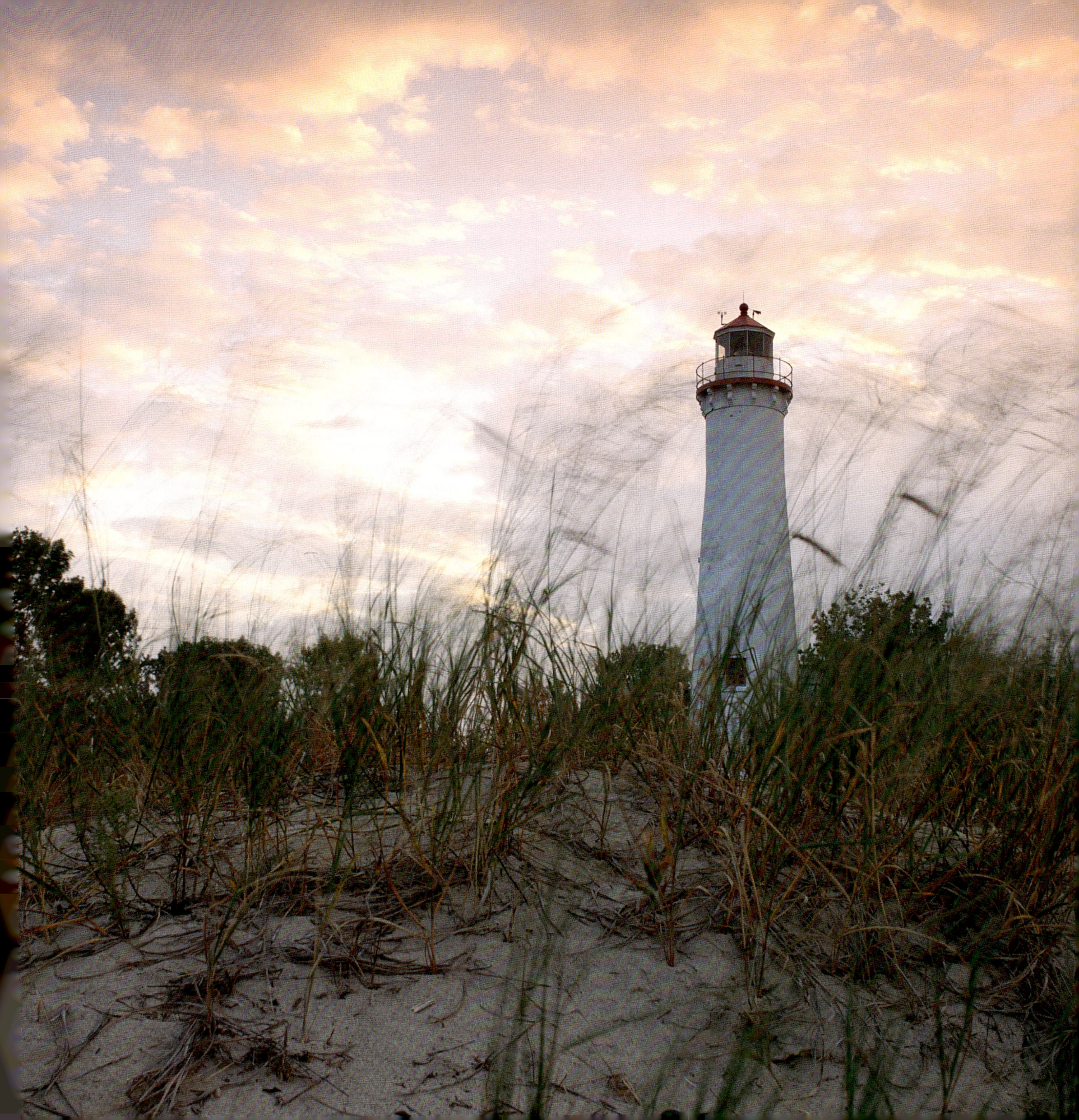

THUNDER BAY ISLAND   *Est. 1832 Lake Huron*

Point Iroquois · Est. 1855 Lake Superior

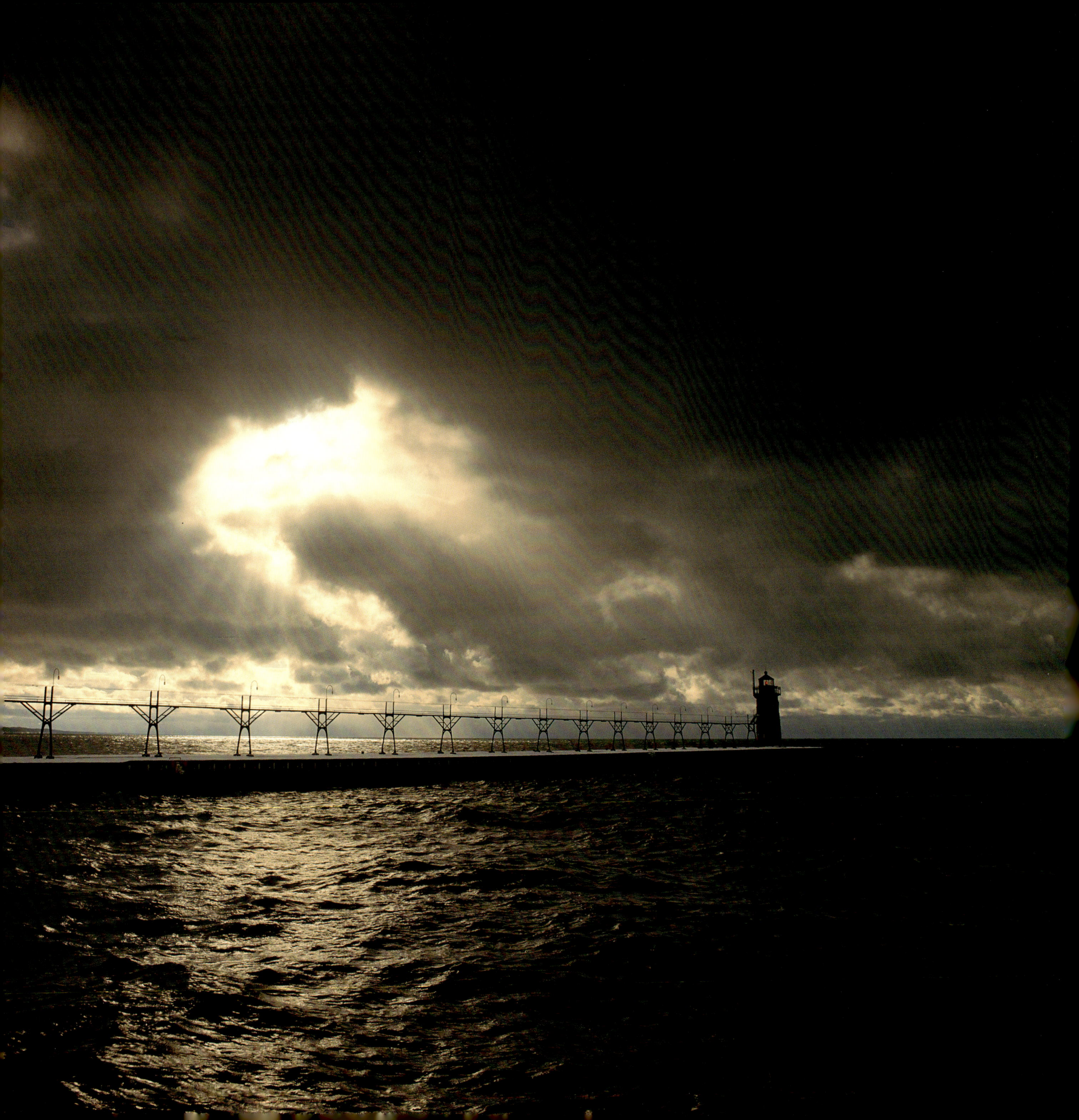

Herring Gull ▲ *Granite Island, Lake Superior*

South Haven ◄ *Est. 1872 Lake Michigan*

POINT IROQUOIS ▲ *Est. 1855 Lake Superior*

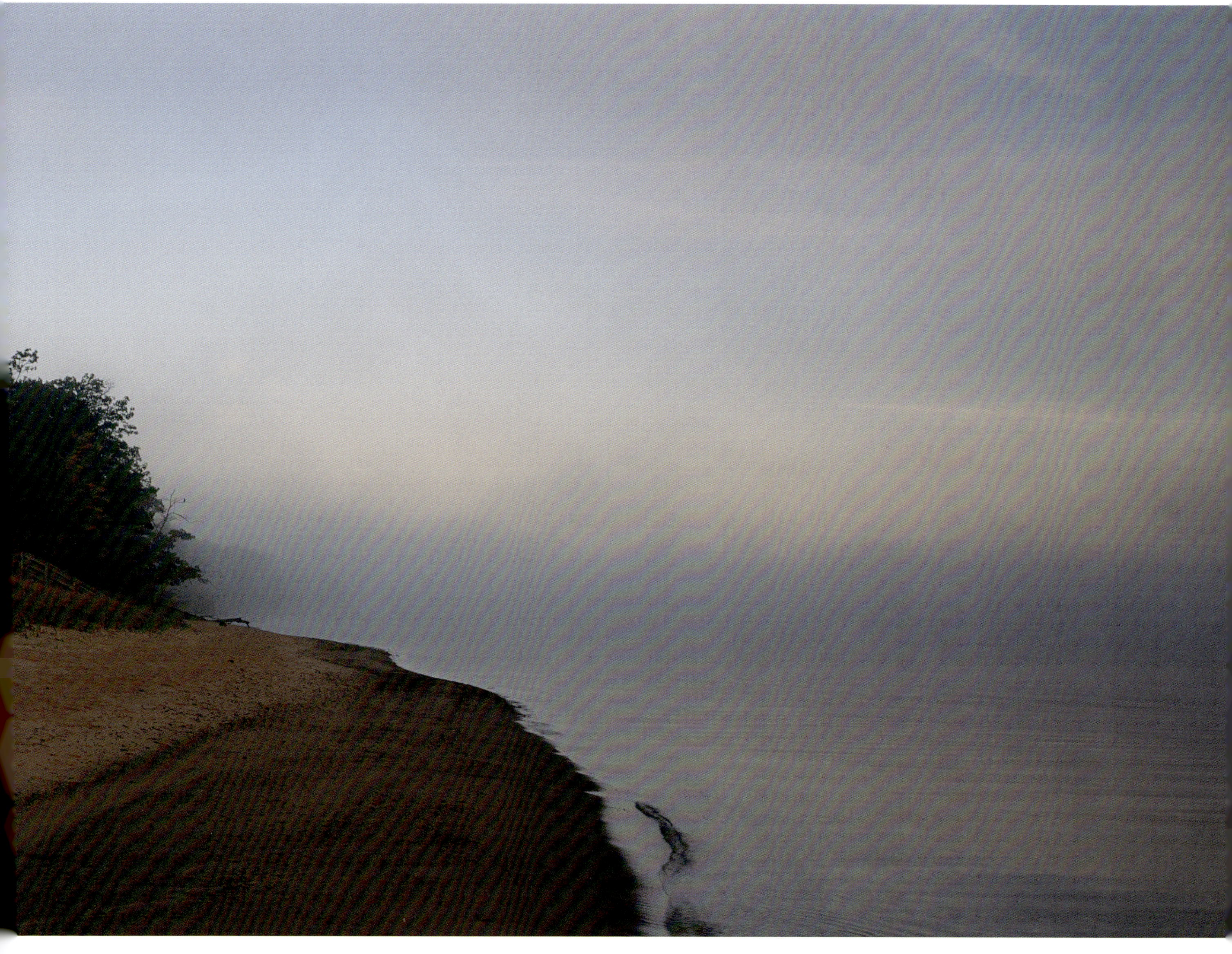

GULL ROCK   ▲   *Est. 1867 Lake Superior*

Agates in the Shallows △ *Point Iroquois, Lake Superior*

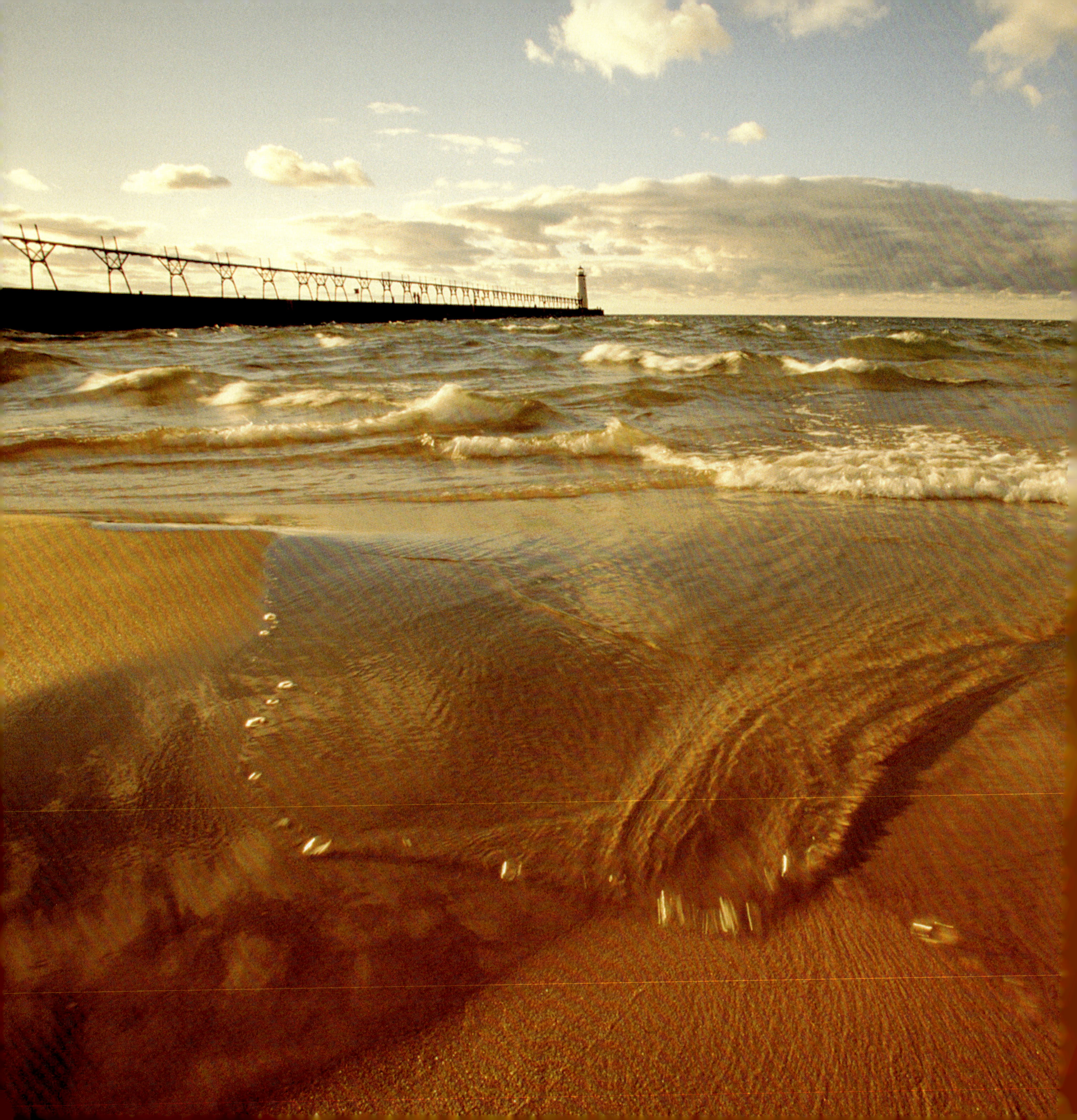

Old Mission ▲ *Est. 1870 Lake Michigan*

Manistee North Pierhead ◄ *Est. 1875 Lake Michigan*

GRAND ISLAND EAST CHANNEL   △   *Est. 1868 Lake Superior*

GRANITE ISLAND ▲ *Est. 1868 Lake Superior*

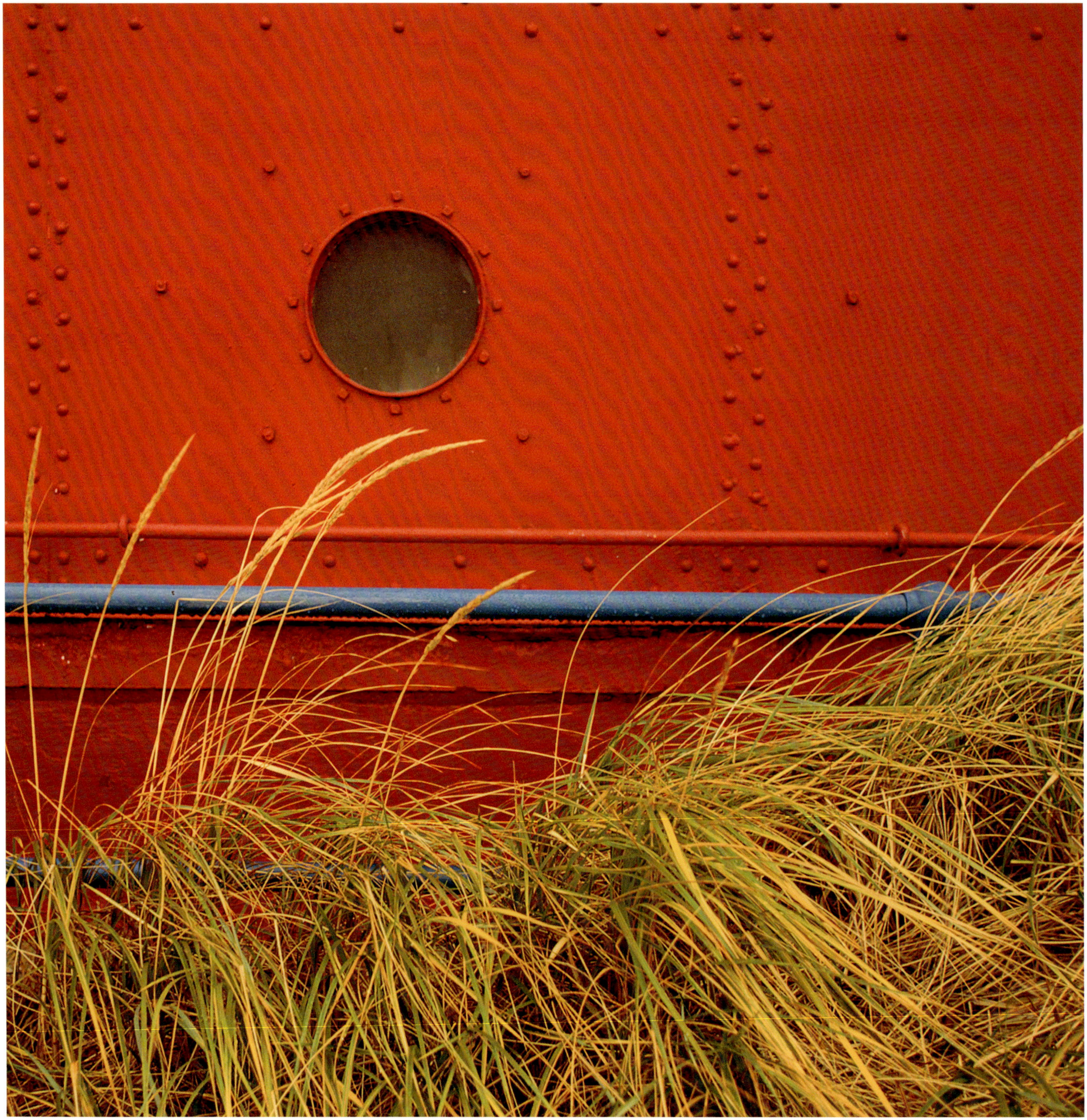

WHITEFISH POINT ◢ *Est. 1849 Lake Superior*

HOLLAND ◂ *Est. 1872 Lake Michigan*

ROUND ISLAND ▲ *Est. 1896 Lake Huron*

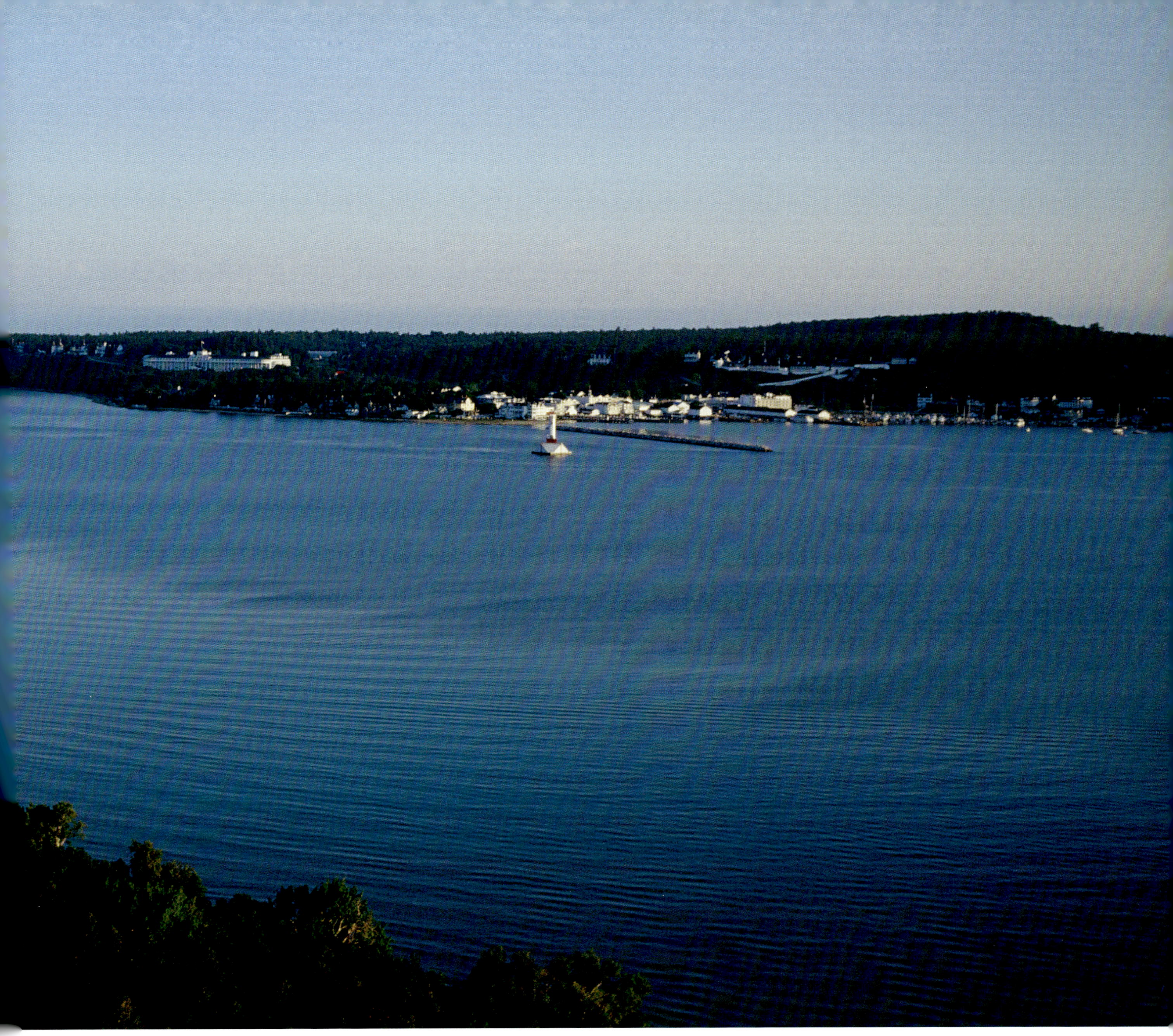

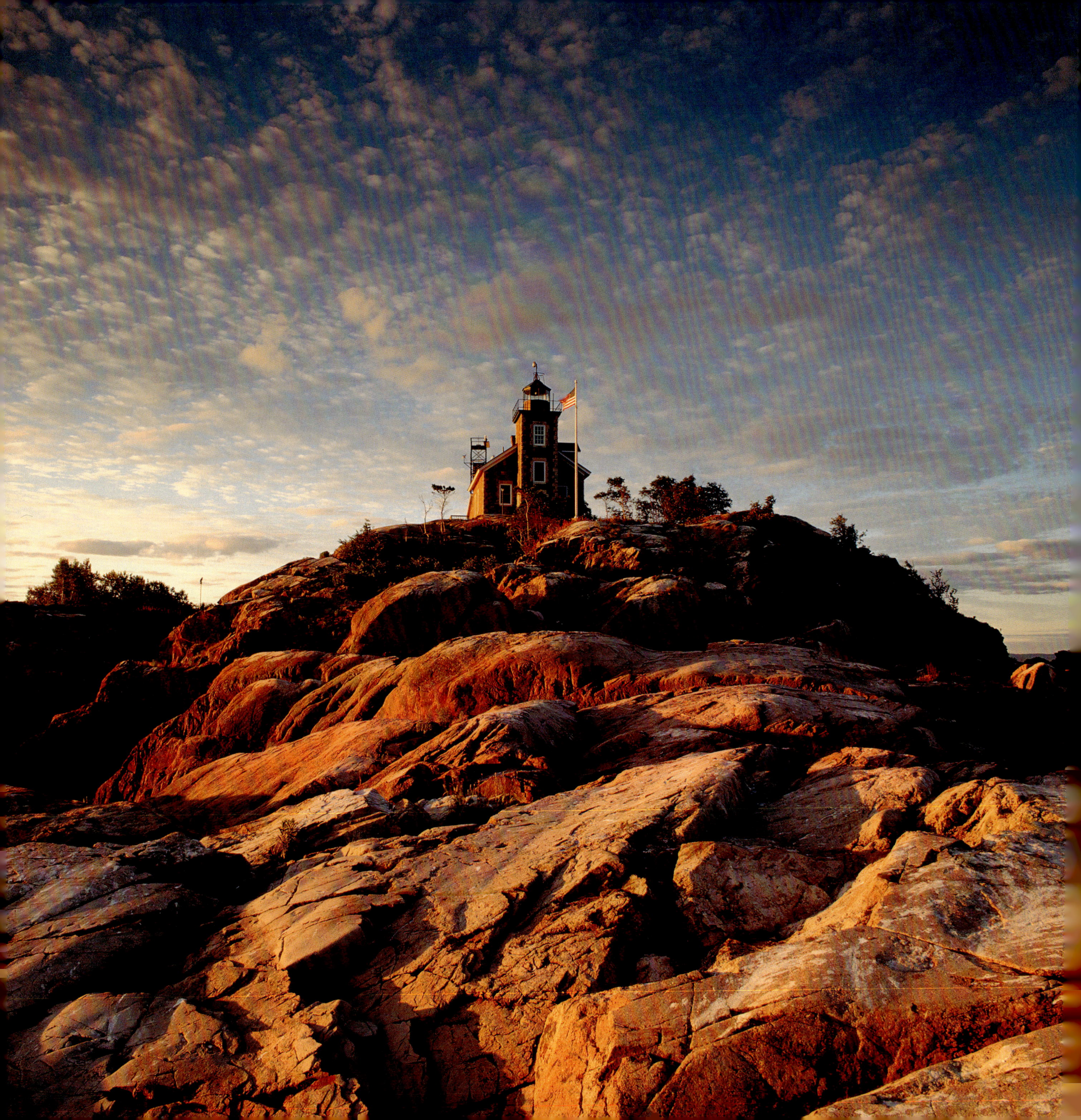

GRAND ISLAND OLD NORTH ◢ *Est. 1855 Lake Superior*

GRANITE ISLAND ◂ *Est. 1868 Lake Superior*

Port Sanilac △ *Est. 1886 Lake Huron*

Big Bay ▷ *Est. 1896 Lake Superior*

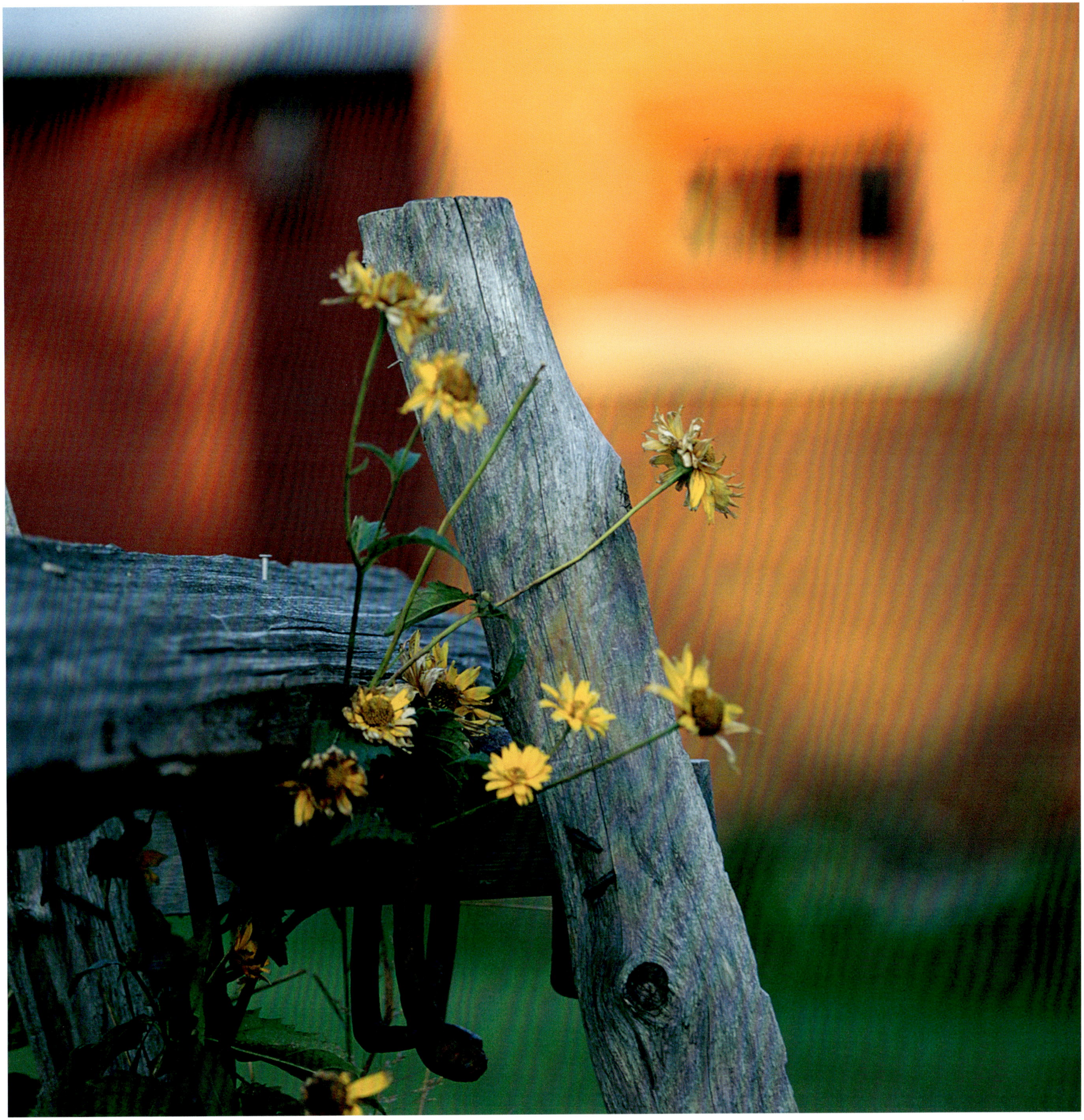

St. Helena Island ▲ *Est. 1873 Lake Michigan*

MENDOTA (BETE GRISE) ▲ *Est. 1870 Lake Superior*

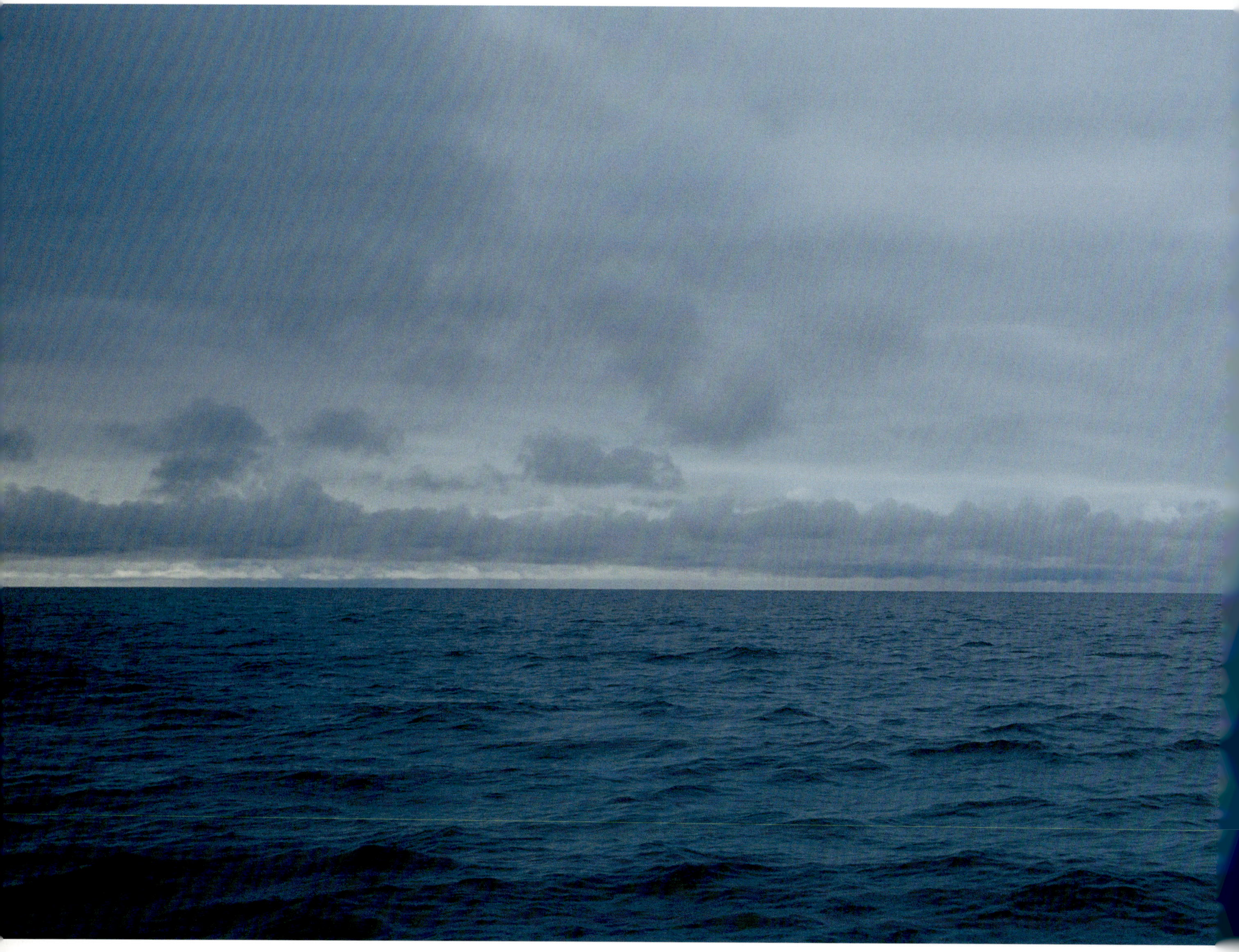

GULL ROCK *Est. 1867 Lake Superior*

DRIFTWOOD AT SUNRISE *Ludington, Lake Michigan*

POINT IROQUOIS   ▲   *Est. 1855 Lake Superior*

MUSKEGON SOUTH PIERHEAD △ *Est. 1851 Lake Michigan*

TAWAS POINT ▷ *Est. 1853 Lake Huron*

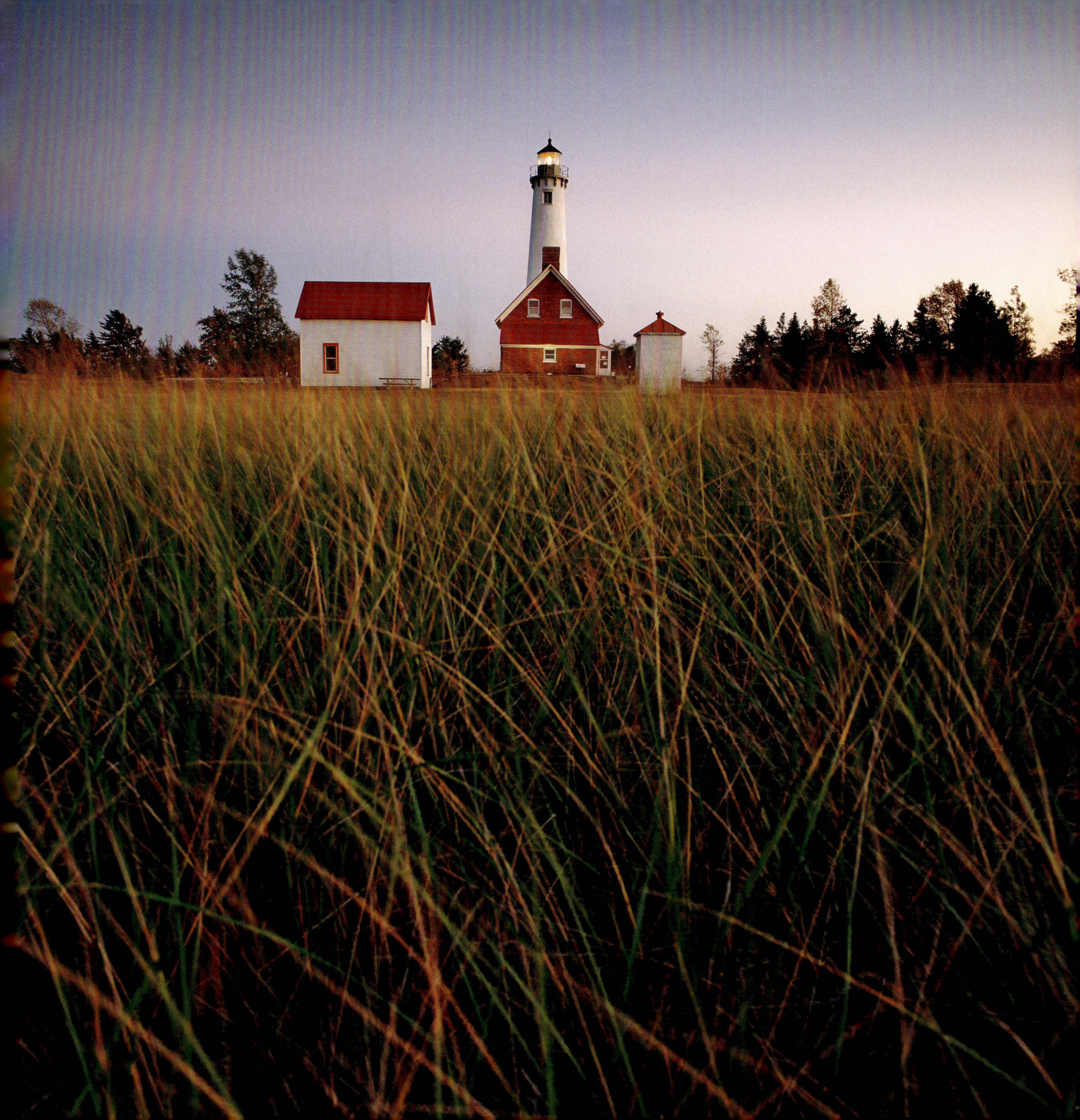

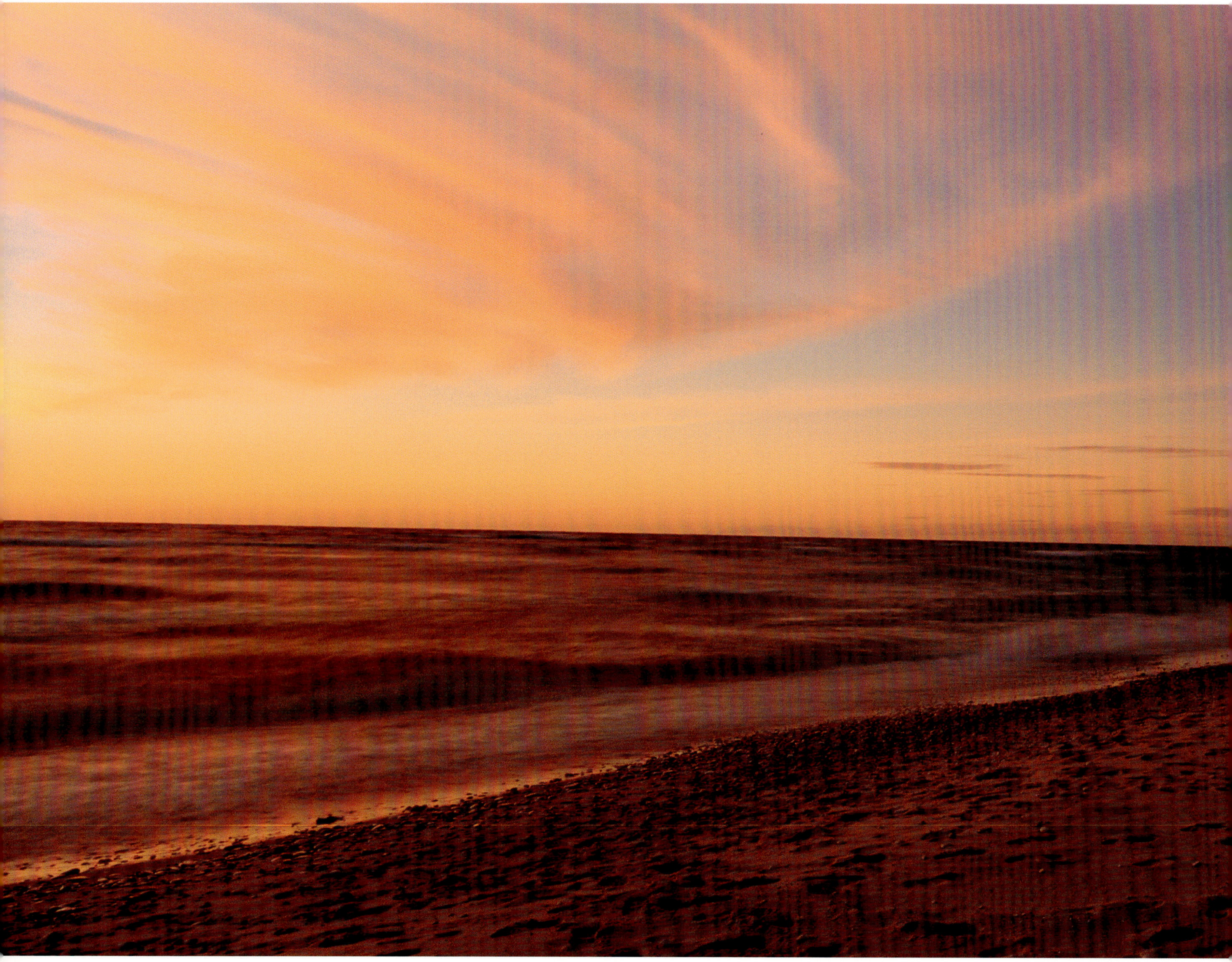

POINT BETSIE ▲ *Est. 1858 Lake Michigan*

WHITEFISH POINT ▲ *Est. 1849 Lake Superior*

WHITEFISH POINT ⚓ *Est. 1849 Lake Superior*

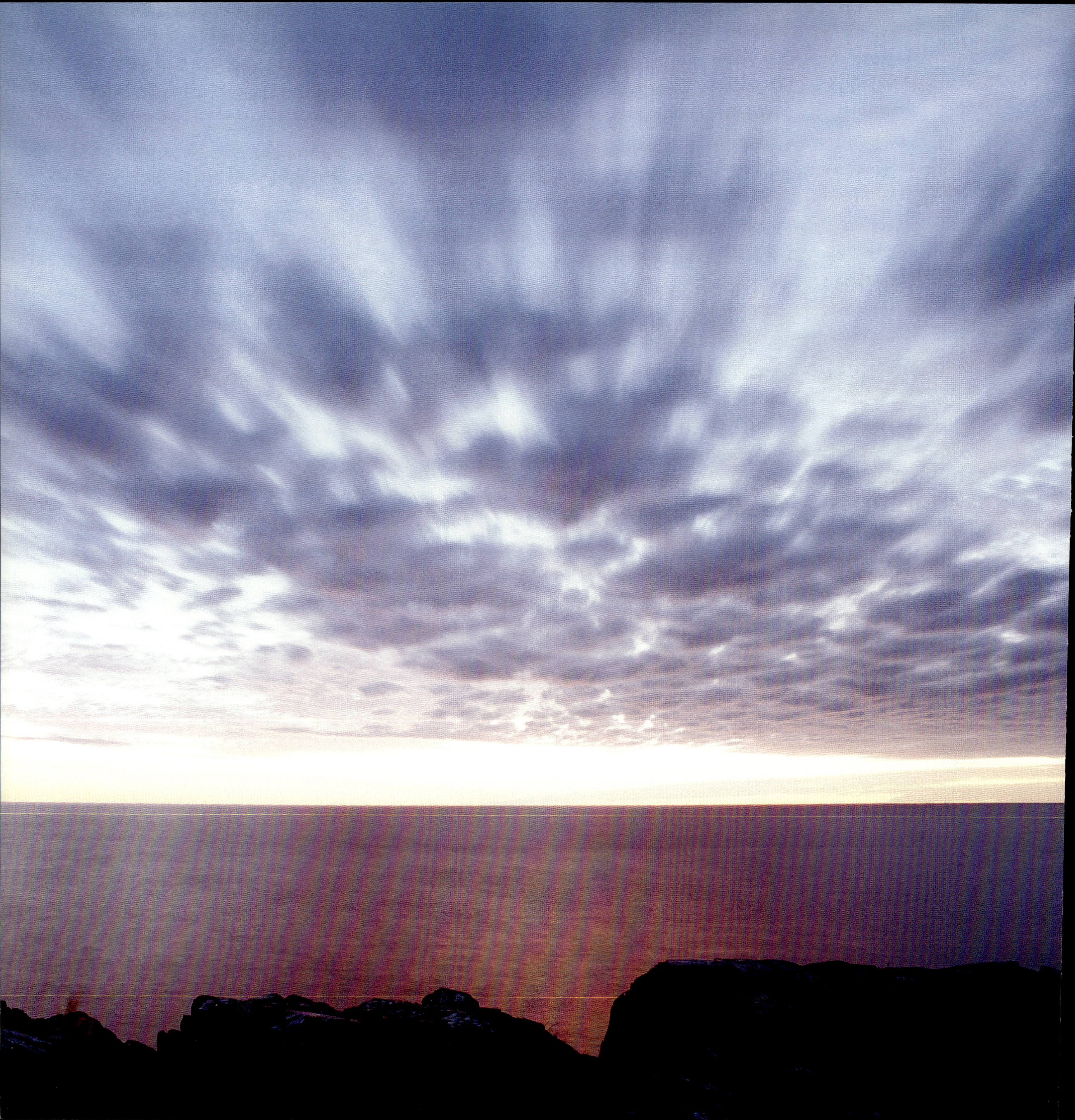

POINTE AUX BARQUE △ *Est. 1848 Lake Huron*

CLOUDS PASSING OVER ◁ *Granite Island, Lake Superior*

BEAVER ISLAND ▲ *Est. 1852 Lake Michigan*

WHITE SHOAL ▶ *Est. 1910 Lake Michigan*

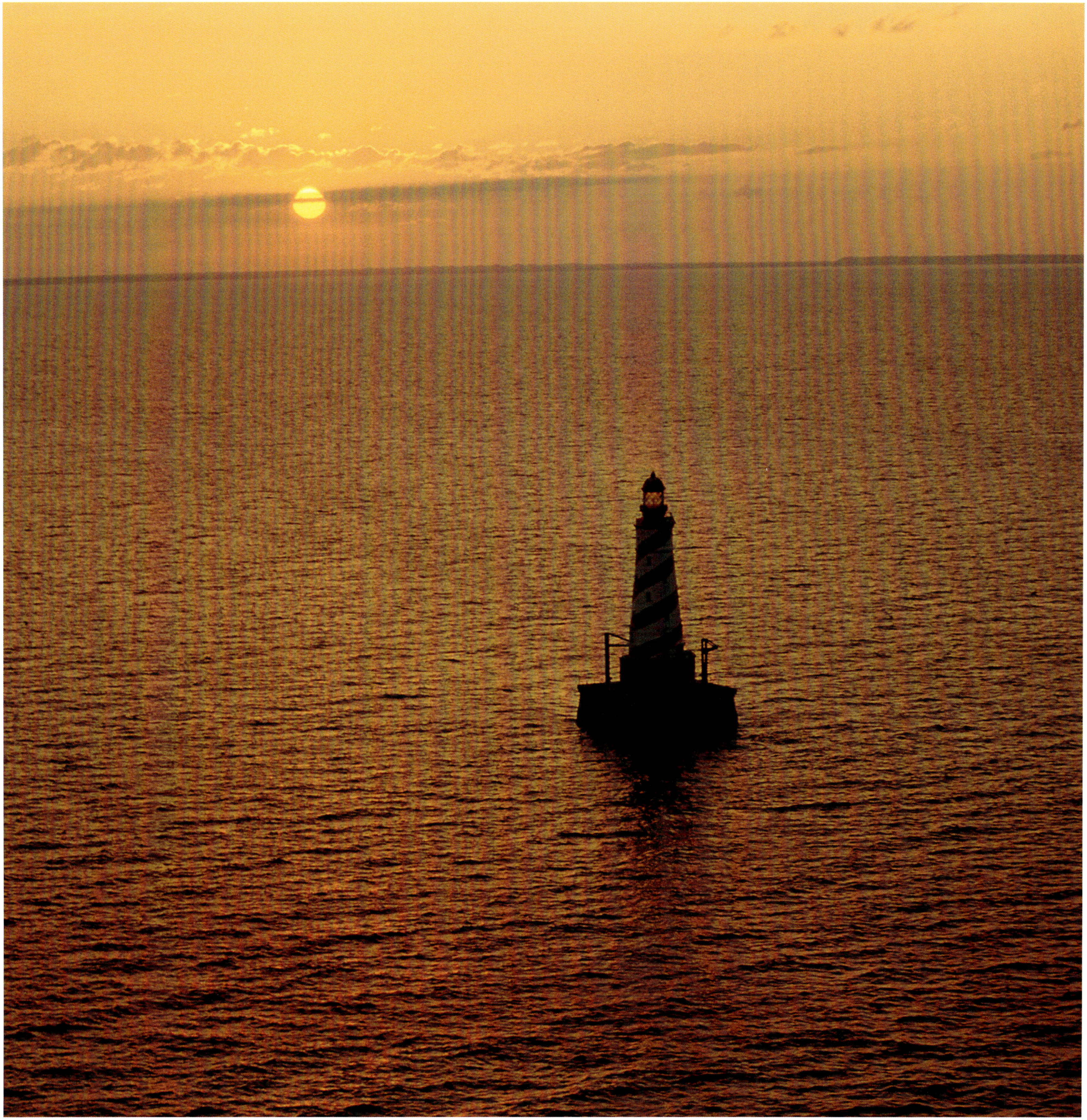

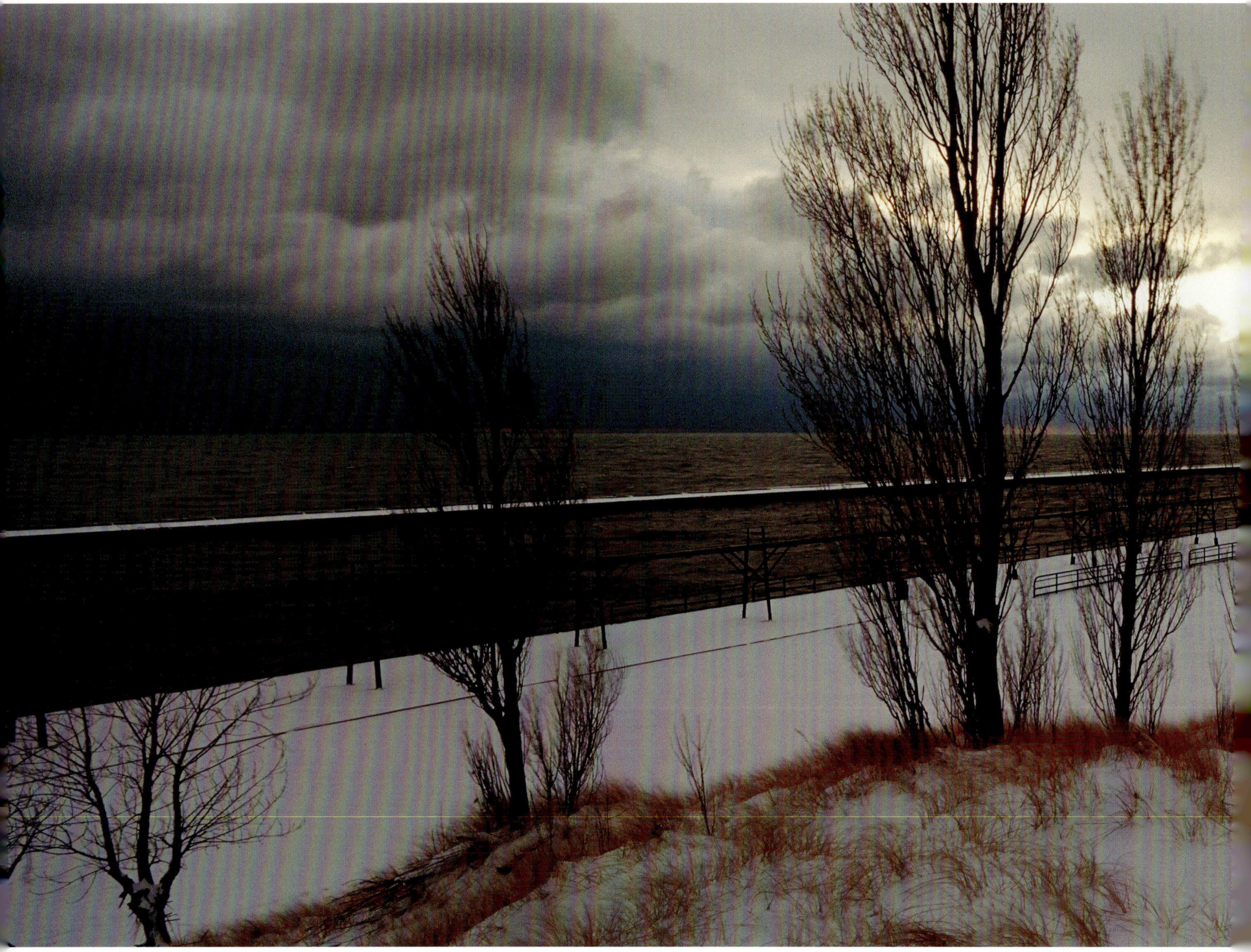

ST. JOSEPH NORTH PIER ▲ *Est. 1832 Lake Michigan*

RECORD OF FOG-SIGNAL

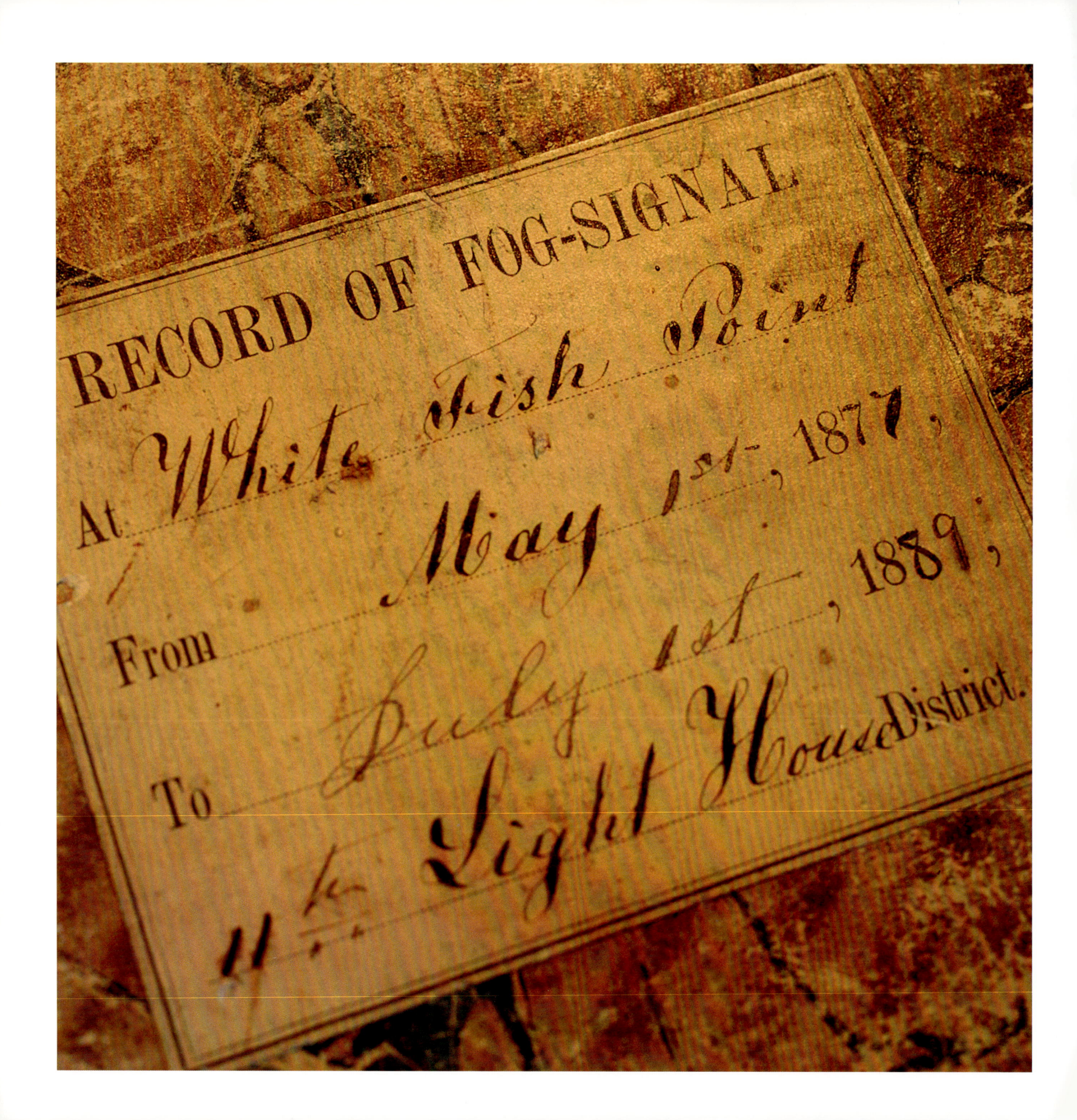

At White Fish Point

From May 1st, 1877,

To July 1st, 1889,

11th Light House District.

GRAND TRAVERSE ⊿ *Est. 1853 Lake Michigan*

WHITEFISH POINT ⊲ *Est. 1848 Lake Superior*

GRANITE ISLAND △ *Est. 1868 Lake Superior*

St. Helena Island ▲ *Est. 1873 Lake Michigan*

GRAND TRAVERSE △ *Est. 1852 Lake Michigan*

SEUL CHOIX POINTE ▷ *Est. 1895 Lake Michigan*

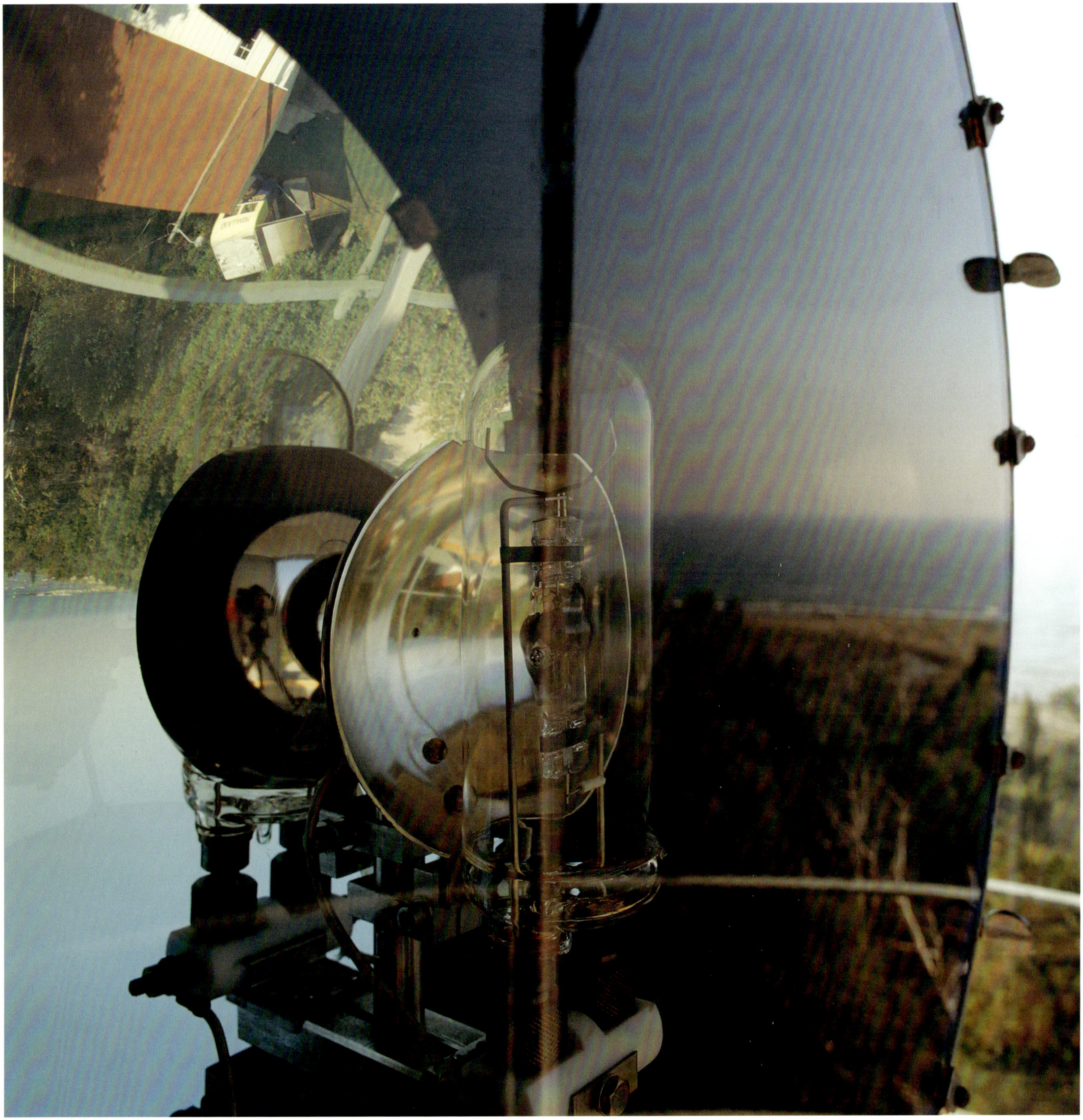

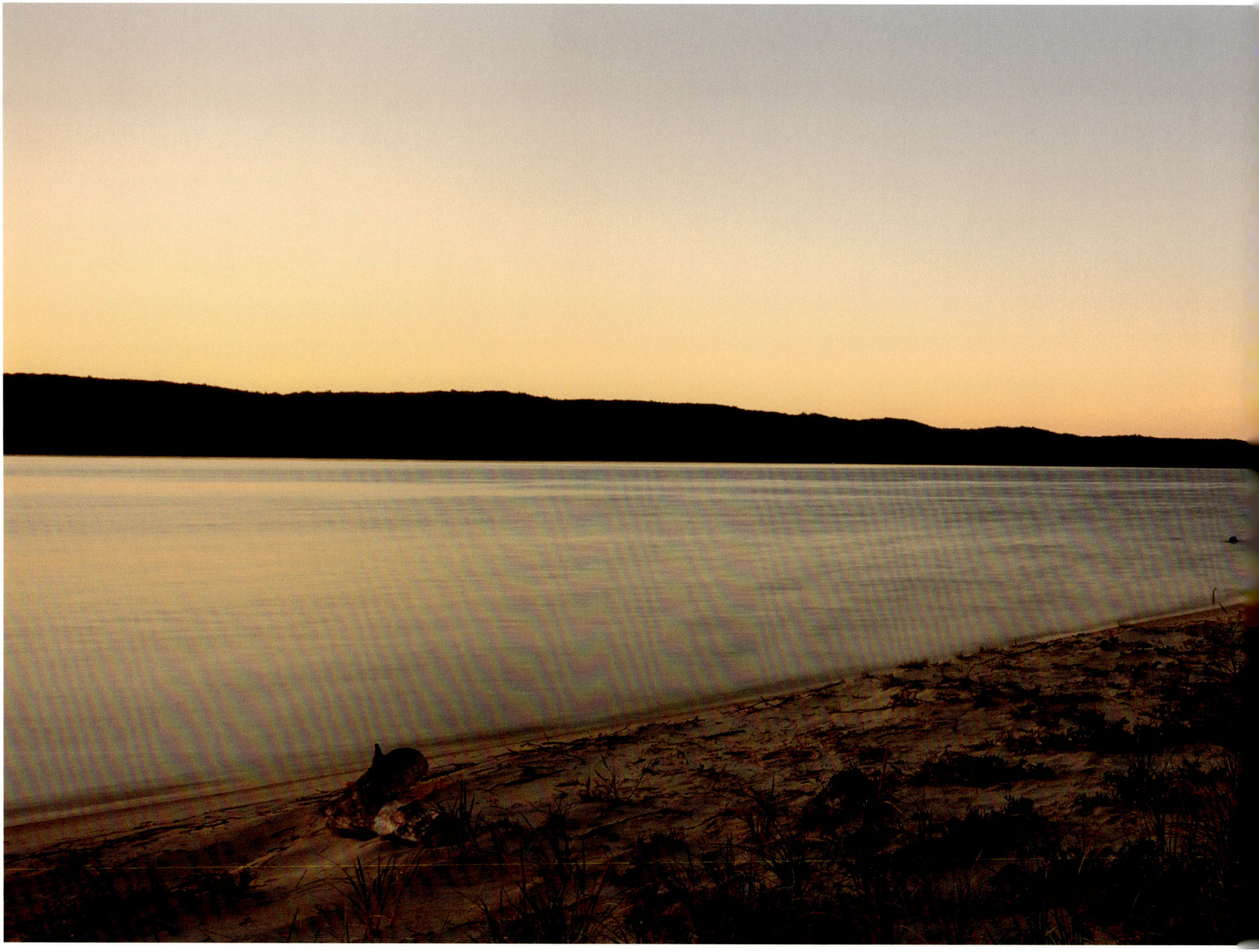

GRAND ISLAND EAST CHANNEL ▲ *Est. 1868 Lake Superior*

EAGLE HARBOR ▲ *Est. 1851 Lake Superior*

GRAND HAVEN ▲ *Est. 1839 Lake Michigan*

Thunder Bay Island   ▲   *Est. 1832 Lake Huron*

GRANITE ISLAND   ▲   *Est. 1868 Lake Superior*

THUNDER BAY ISLAND   ▲   *Est. 1832 Lake Huron*

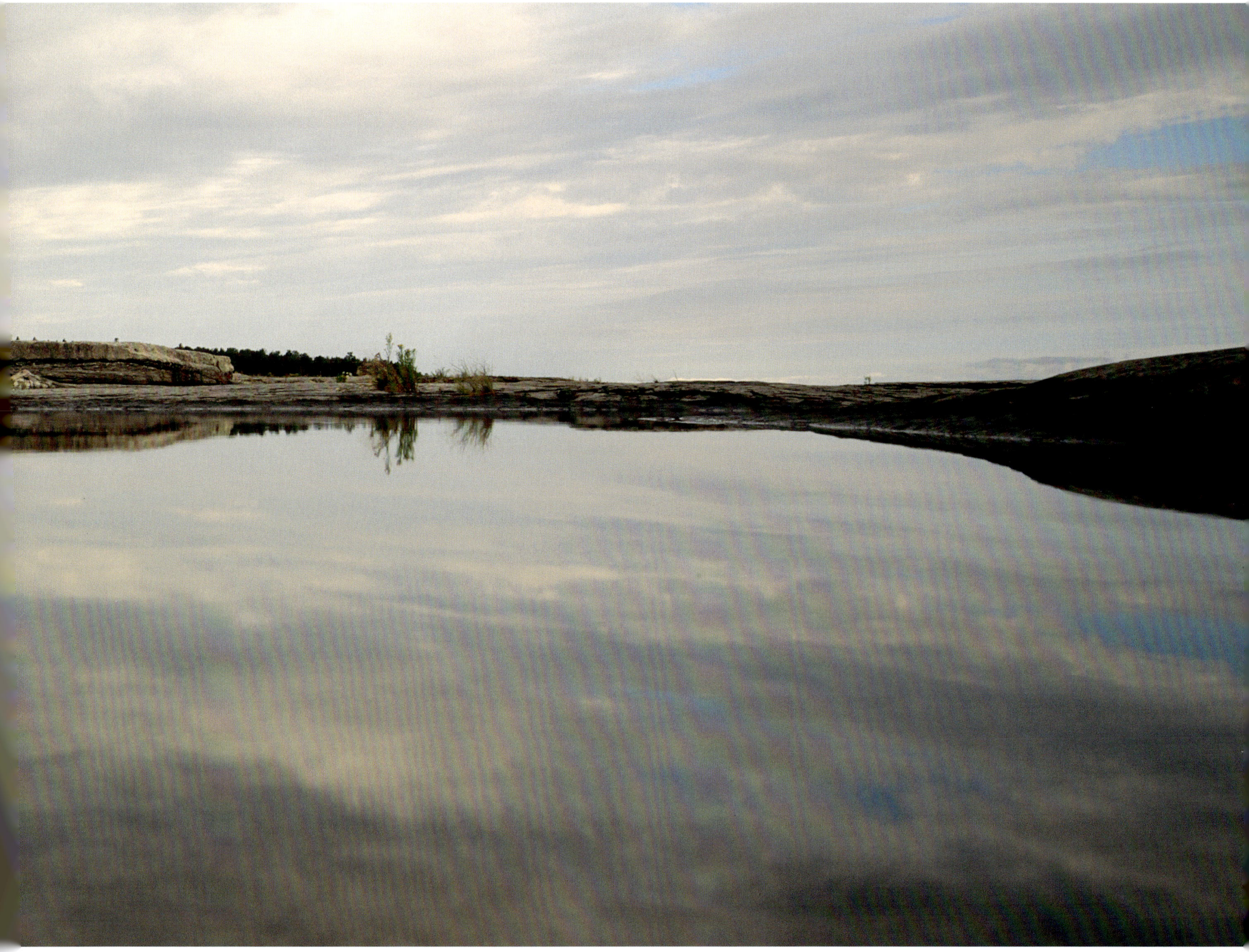

POINT IROQUOIS ▲ *Est. 1855 Lake Superior*

OLD PRESQUE ISLE ▲ *Est. 1840 Lake Huron*

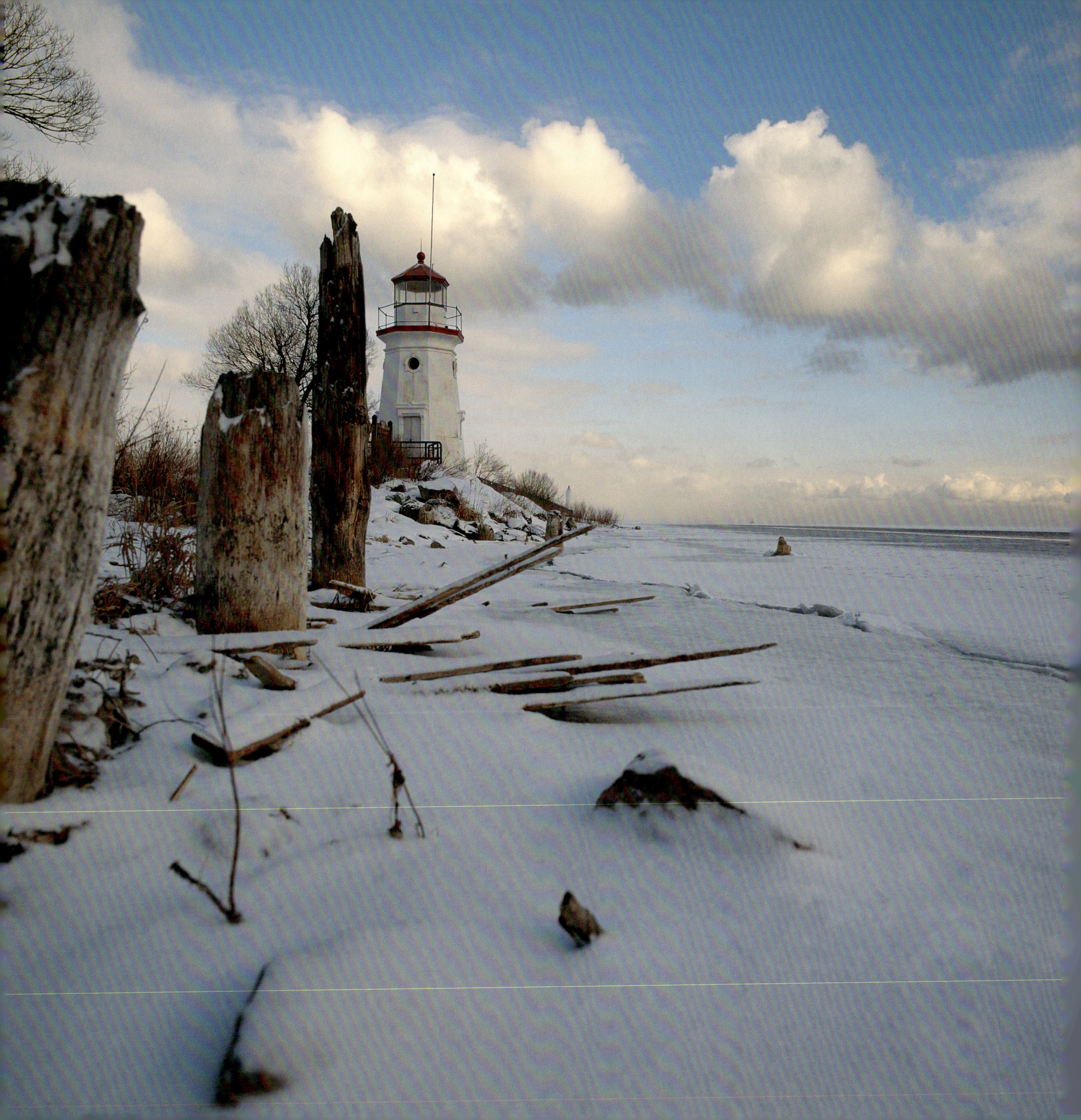

ST. JOSEPH NORTH PIER ◭ *Est. 1832 Lake Michigan*
CHEBOYGAN CRIB LIGHT ◀ *Est. 1884 Lake Huron*

Manistique East Breakwater   Est. 1915 Lake Michigan

ROUND ISLAND △ *Est. 1896 Lake Huron*

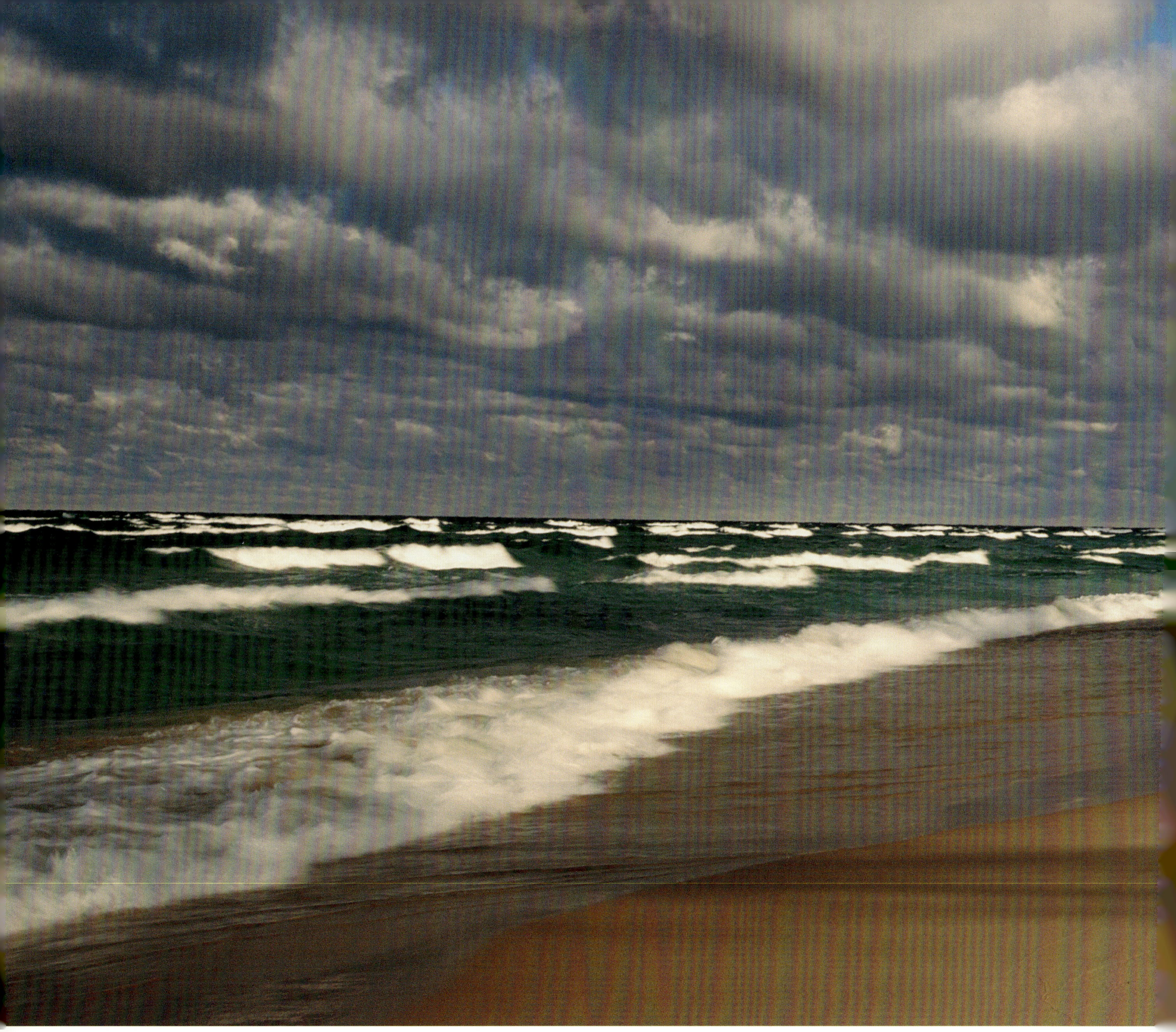

POINT BETSIE ▲ *Est. 1858 Lake Michigan*

ROCK HARBOR, ISLE ROYALE ▲ *Est. 1855 Lake Superior*

THE SHIPWRECK *Morazan* ▲ *South Manitou Island, Lake Michigan*

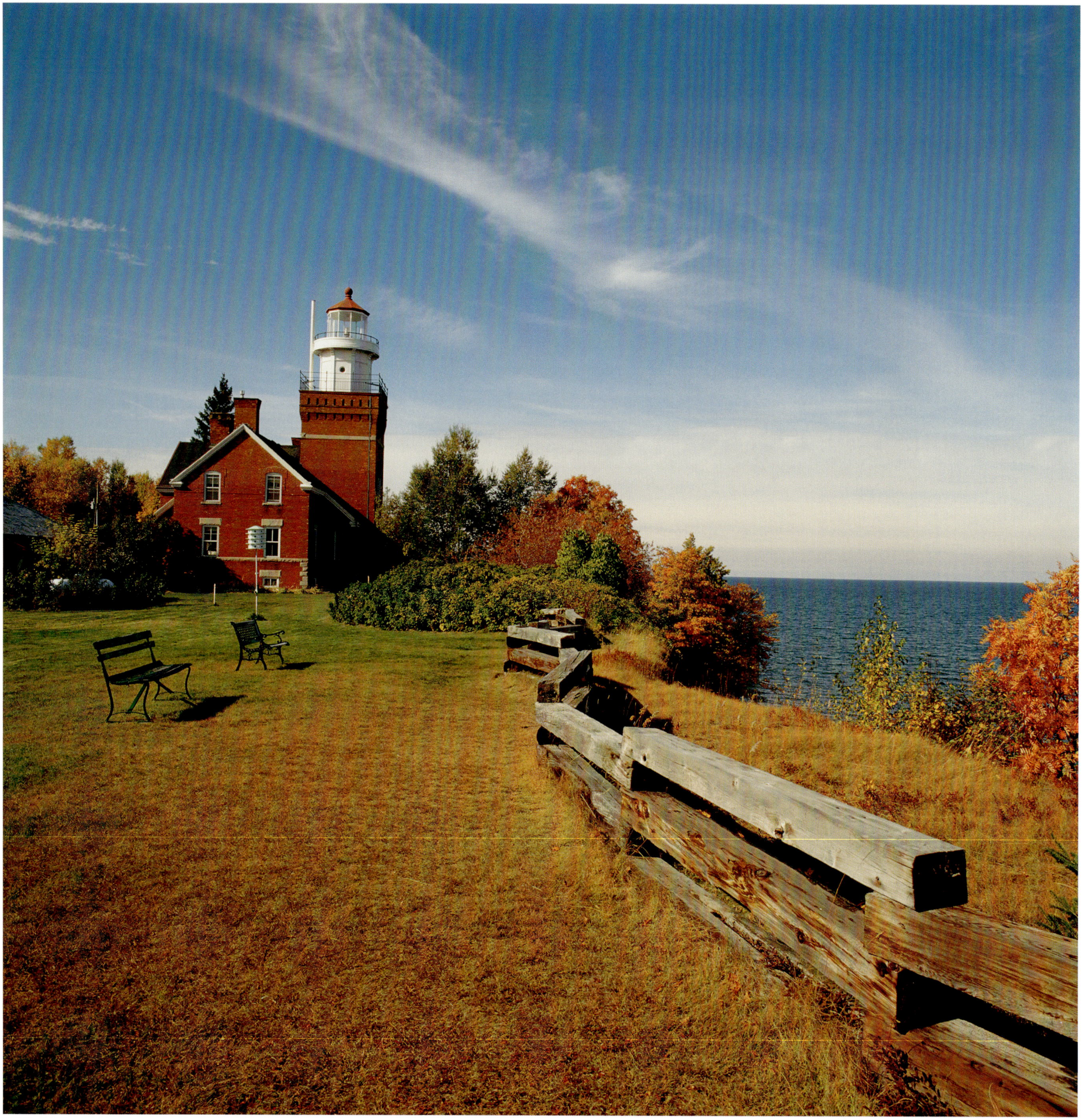

BEAVER ISLAND ◢ *Est. 1851 Lake Michigan*

BIG BAY POINT ◂ *Est. 1896 Lake Superior*

GRANITE ISLAND ▲ *Est. 1868 Lake Superior*

MANISTEE NORTH PIERHEAD ▶ *Est. 1875 Lake Michigan*

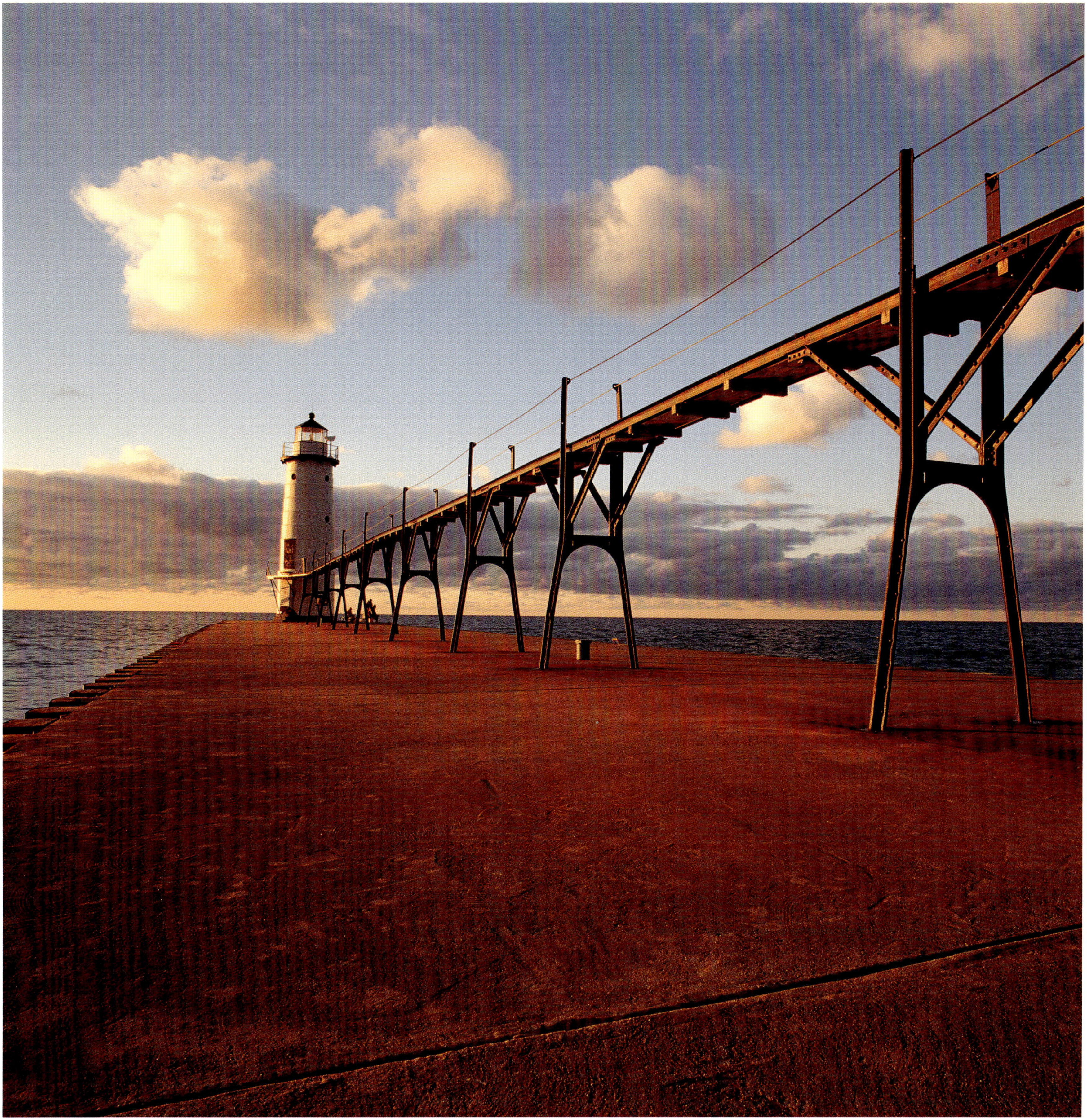

SNOWFENCE INTO INFINITY ▲ *Holland, Lake Michigan*

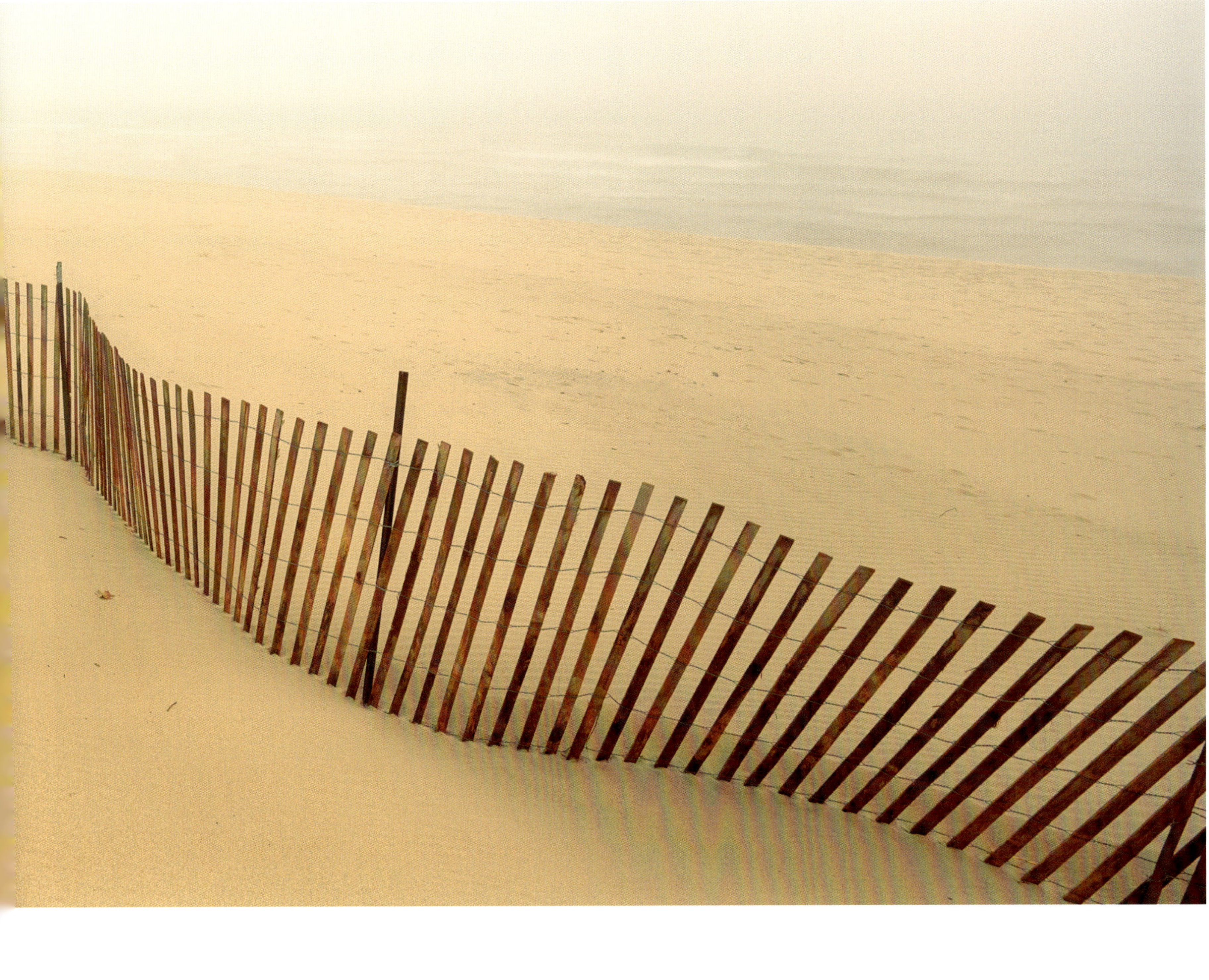

FREIGHTER HEADING WEST ▲ *Point Iroquois, Lake Superior*

MARQUETTE HARBOR LIGHT *Est. 1853 Lake Superior*

DETROIT RIVER △ *Est. 1885 Lake Erie*

Tawas Point *Est. 1853 Lake Huron*

THUNDER BAY ISLAND ▲ *Est. 1832 Lake Huron*

THUNDER BAY ISLAND ▲ *Est. 1832 Lake Huron*

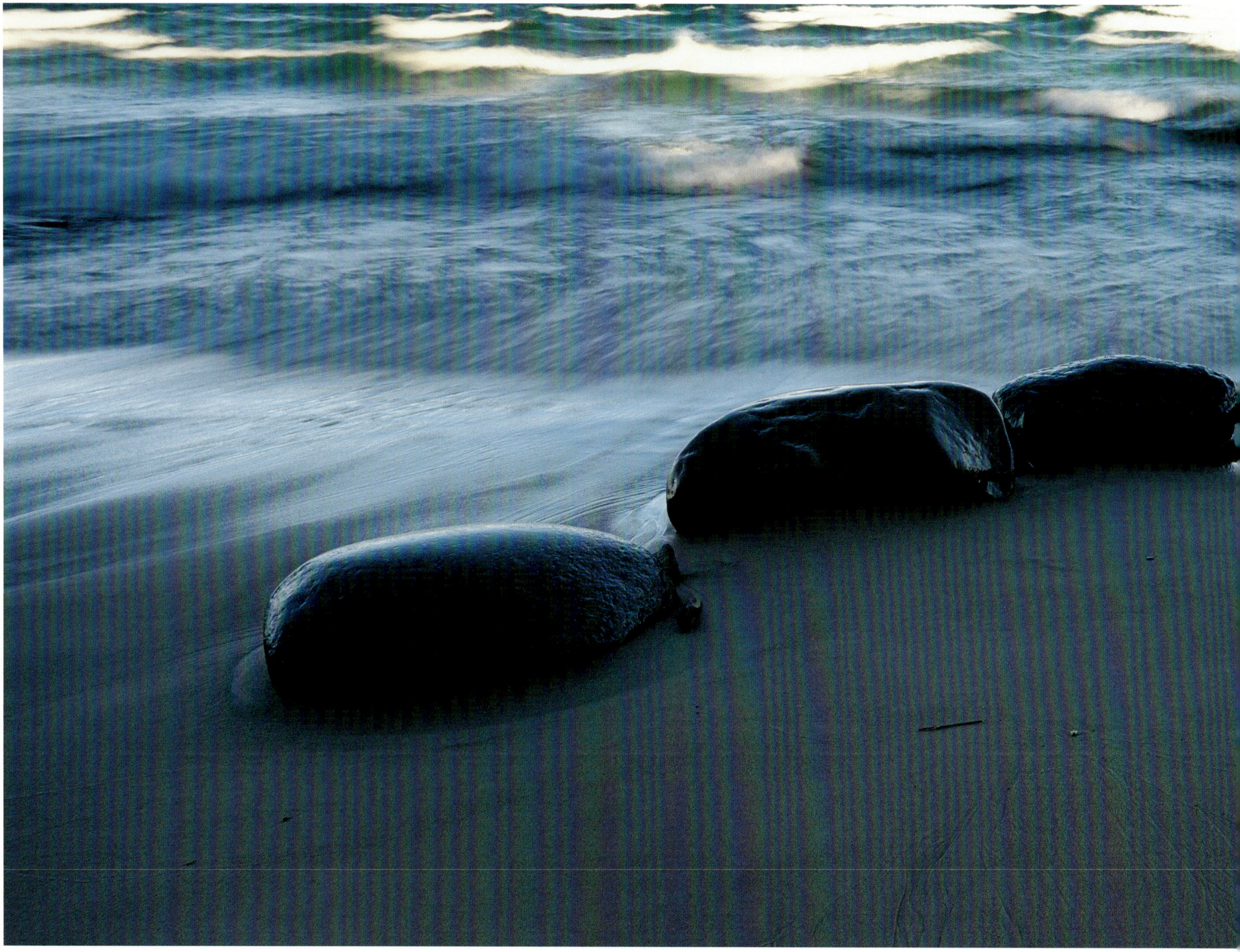

Surf and Stones   ▲   *Pictured Rocks National Lakeshore*

BIG BAY POINT ▲ *Est. 1896 Lake Superior*

AU SABLE POINT ▶ *Est. 1874 Lake Superior*

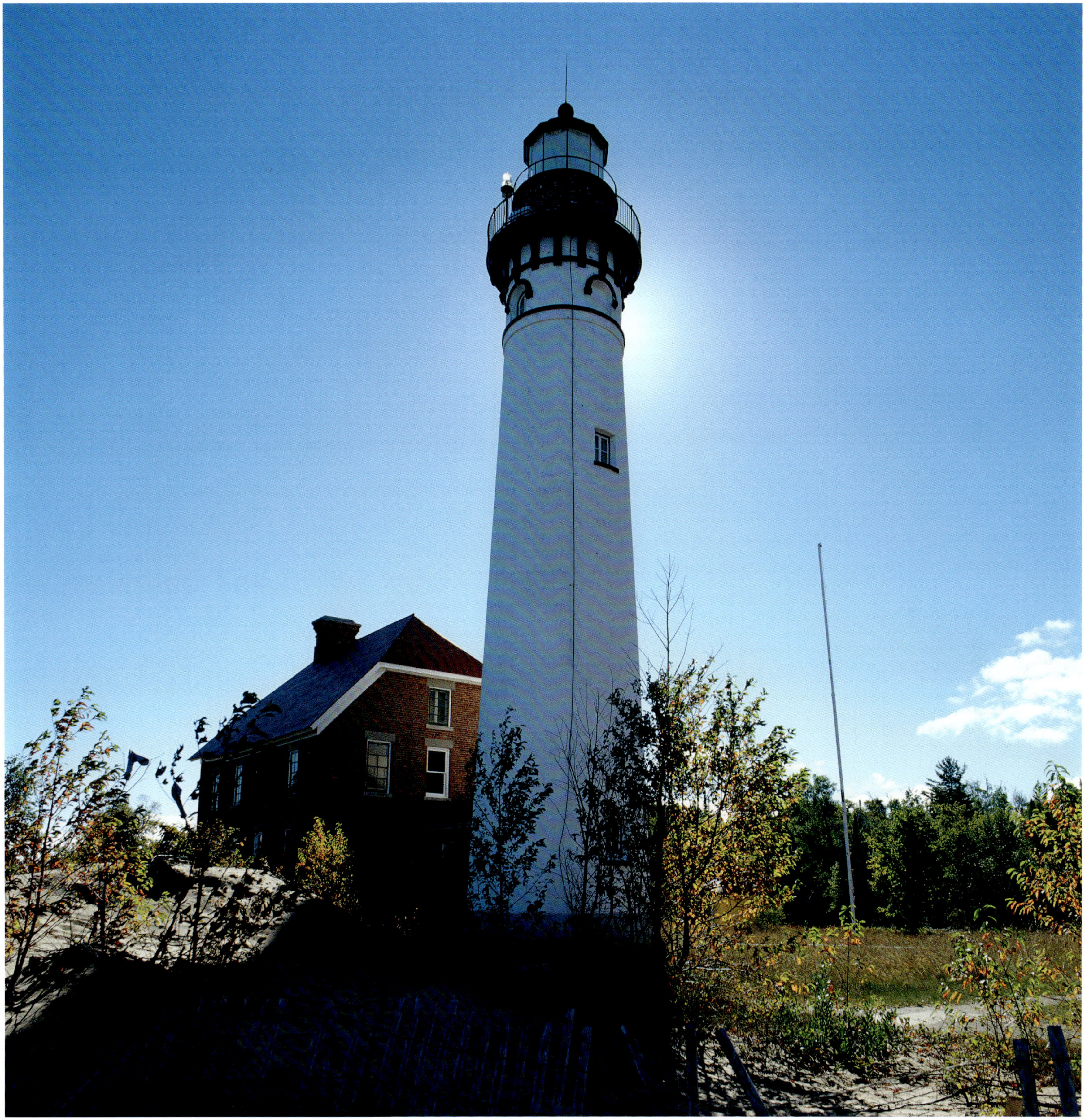

St. Helena Island ▲ Est. 1873 Lake Michigan

FOREST FLOOR ALONG FOOTPATH ▲ *Isle Royale National Park, Lake Superior*

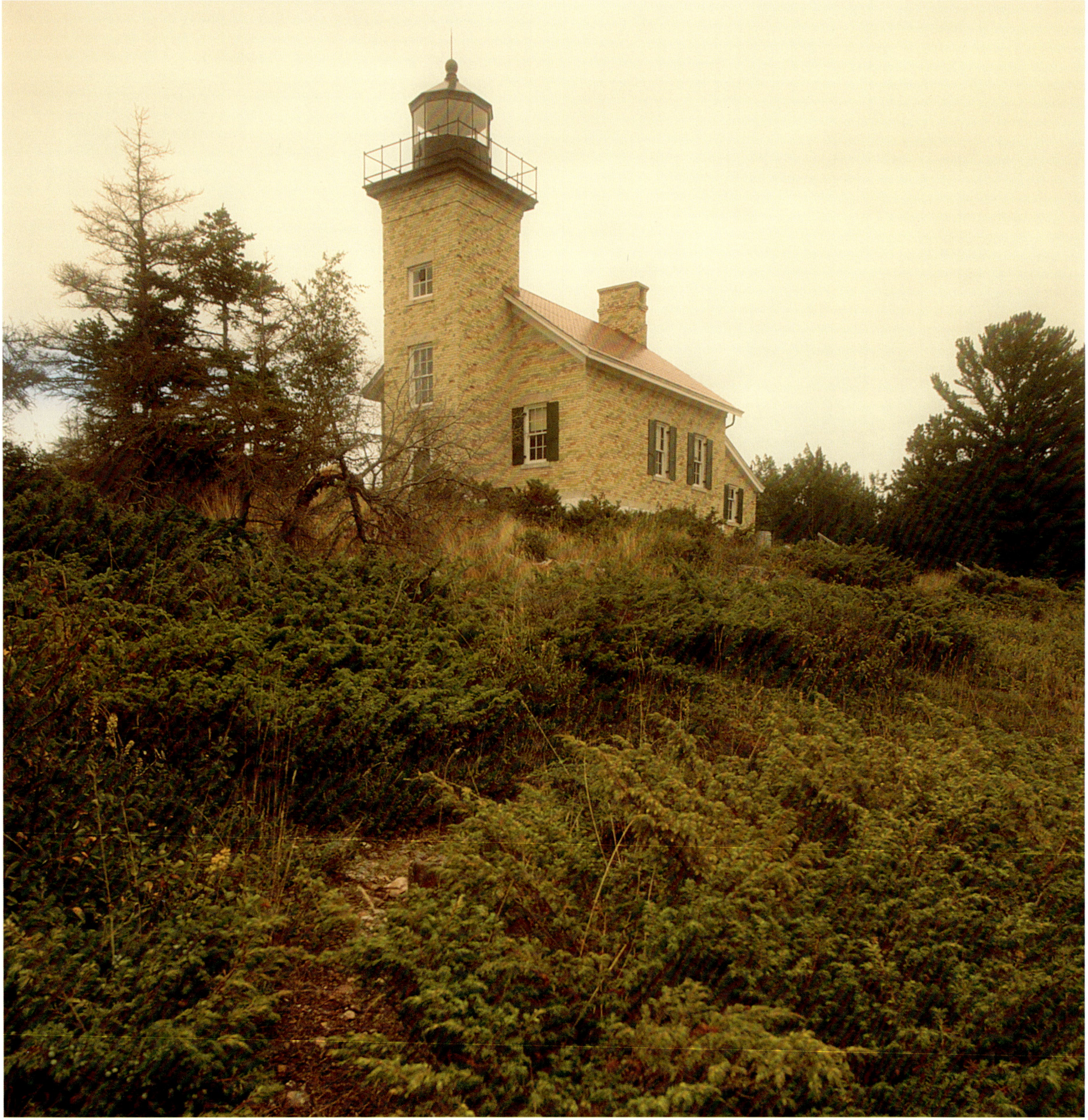

HOLLAND   ◣   *Est. 1872 Lake Michigan*

COPPER HARBOR   ◀   *Est. 1849 Lake Superior*

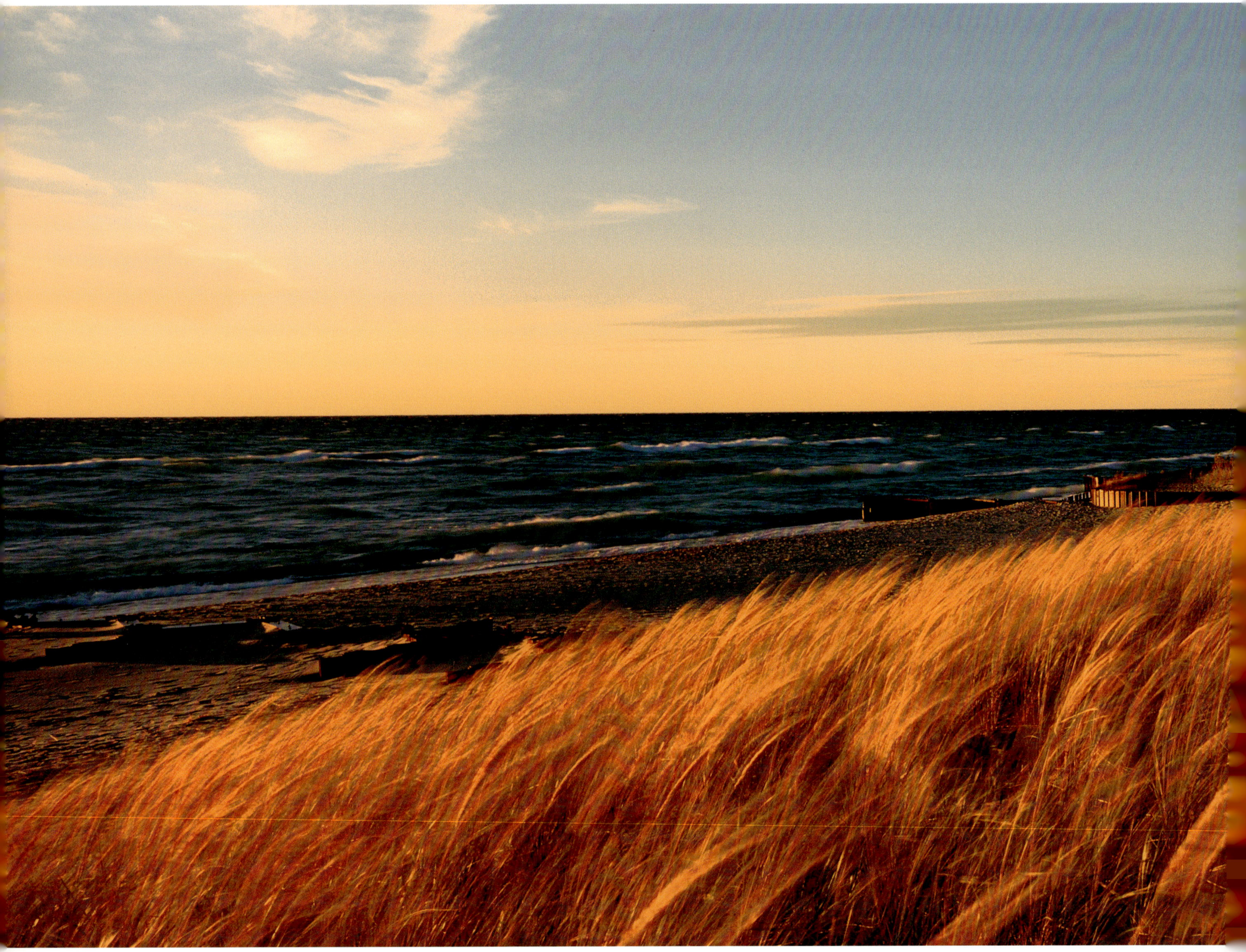

Point Betsie ▲ Est. 1858 Lake Michigan

EAGLE HARBOR ▲ *Est. 1851 Lake Superior*

Waves Along Grand Sable Dunes   ▲   *Pictured Rocks National Lakeshore*

Huron Island △ *Est. 1868 Lake Superior*

Rock Harbor, Isle Royale ▷ *Est. 1855 Lake Superior*

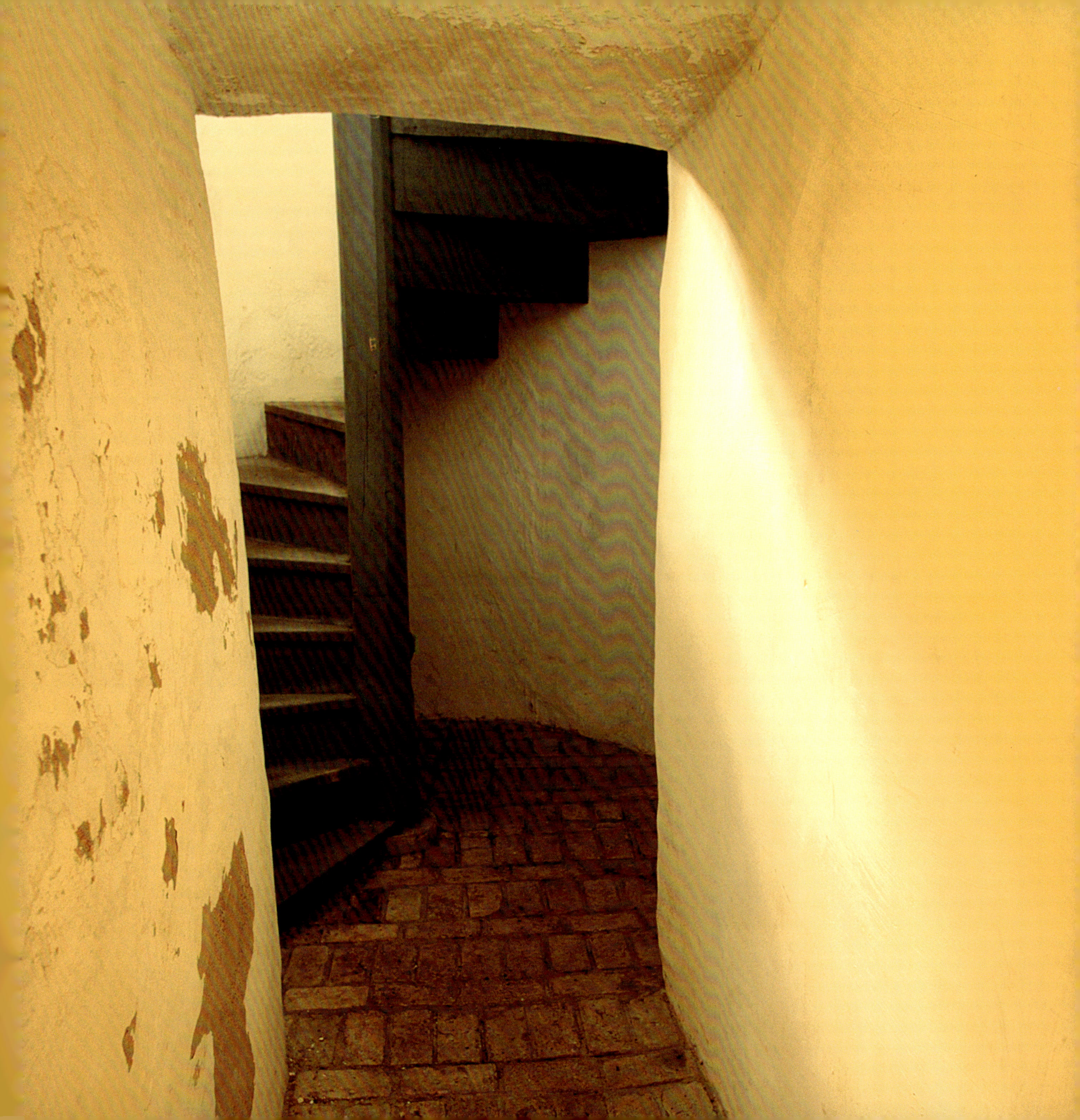

ROCK HARBOR, ISLE ROYALE   ⚴   Est. 1855 Lake Superior

Thunder Bay Island ▲ Est. 1832 Lake Huron

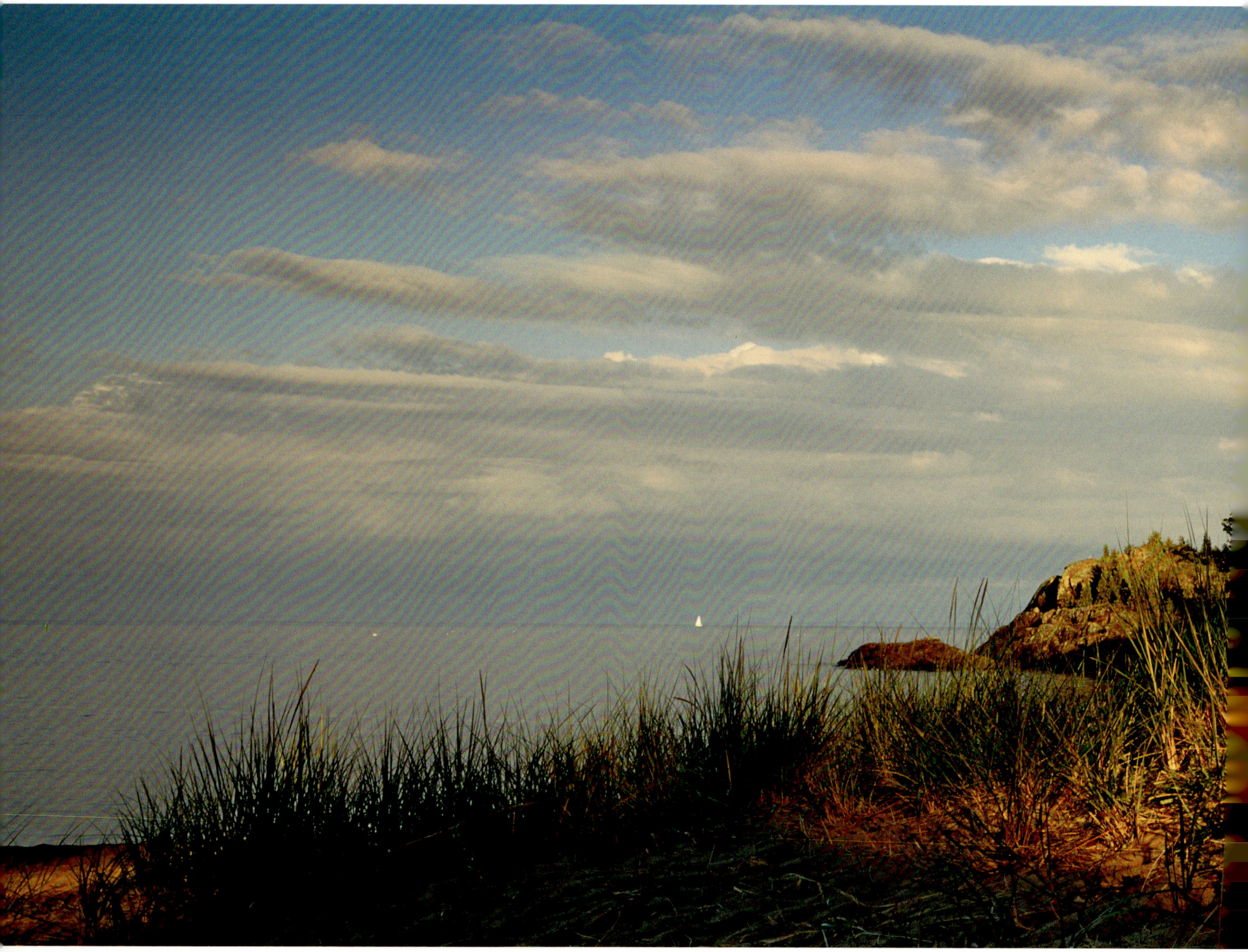

MARQUETTE HARBOR LIGHT ▲ *Est. 1853 Lake Superior*

SKILLAGALEE (ILE AUX GALETS)   ▲   *Est. 1850 Lake Michigan*

Copper Harbor ▲ Est. 1849 Lake Superior

Seul Choix Pointe   Est. 1892 Lake Michigan

BLUFFS ENTERING THE WATER ▲ *Pictured Rocks National Lakeshore*

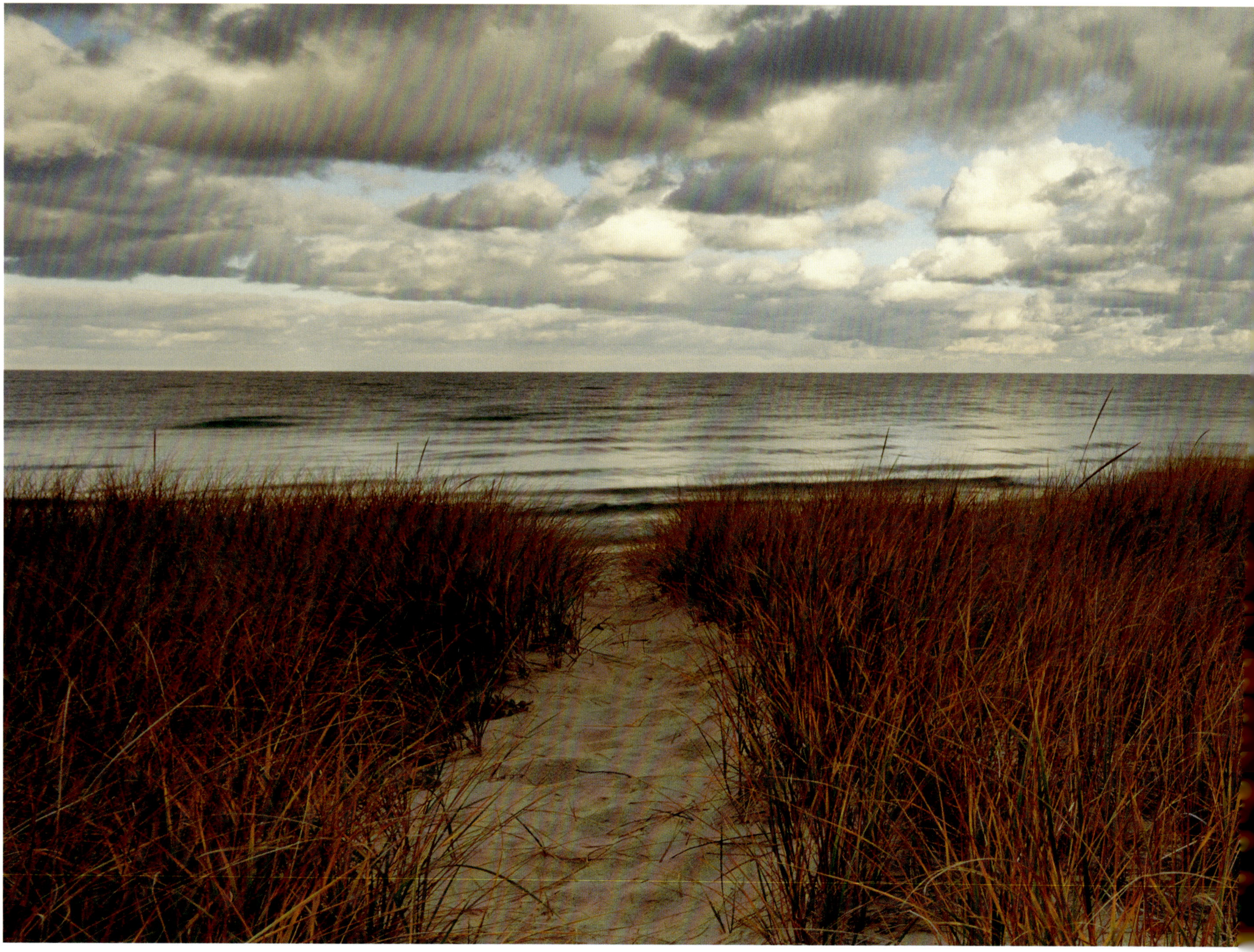

CHARLEVOIX SOUTH PIERHEAD ▲ *Est. 1914 Lake Michigan*

Old Presque Isle ▲ *Est. 1840 Lake Huron*

BIG BAY POINT ⚜ *Est. 1896 Lake Superior*

Huron Island △ *Est. 1868 Lake Superior*

Underwater Rock Formation ▷ *Grand Island, Lake Superior*

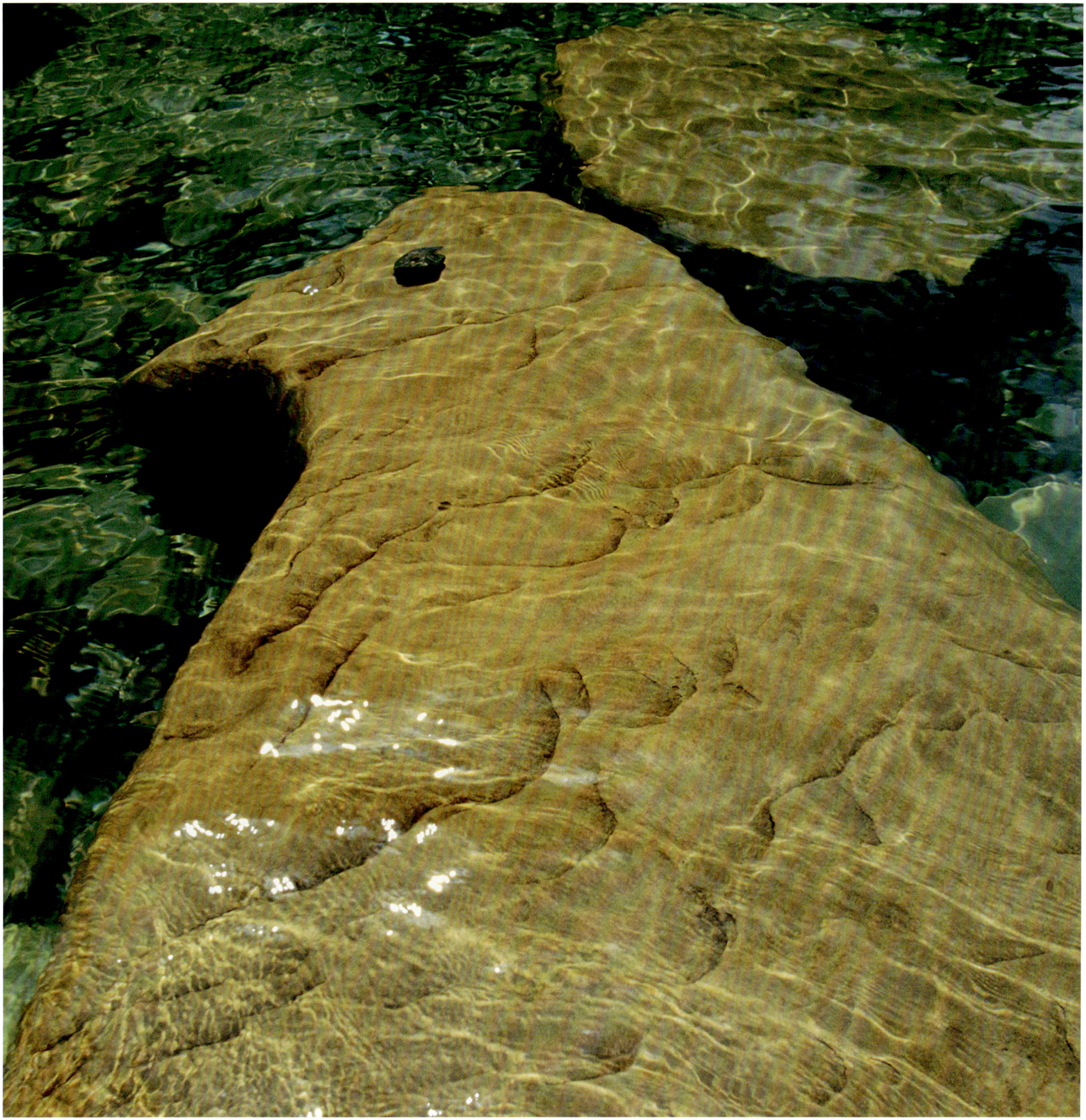

WHITEFISH POINT   A   *Est. 1848 Lake Superior*

Seul Choix Pointe   Est. 1892 Lake Michigan

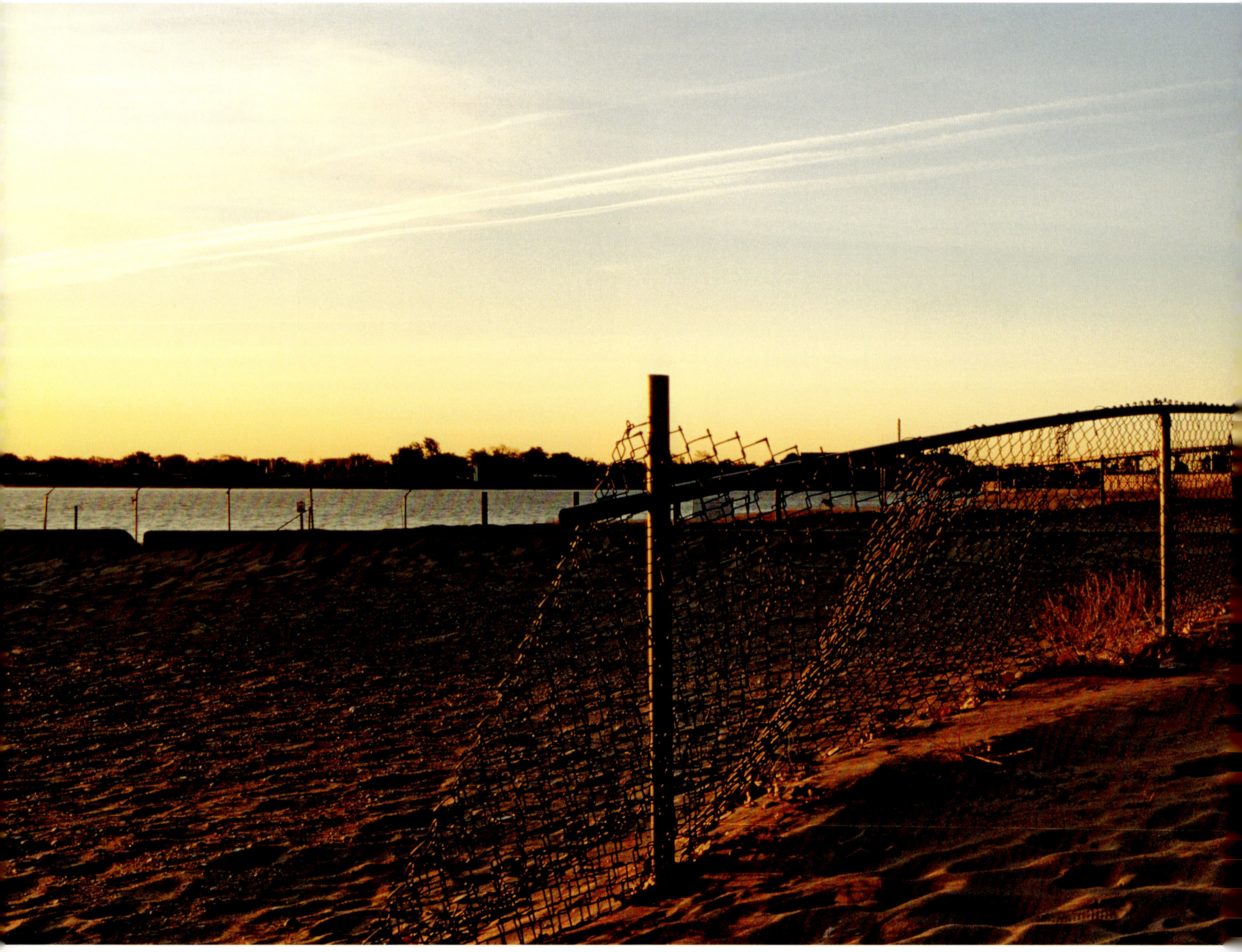

FORT GRATIOT ▲ *Est. 1825 Lake Huron*

ROUND ISLAND ▲ *Est. 1896 Lake Huron*

POINT BETSIE ▲ *Est. 1858 Lake Michigan*

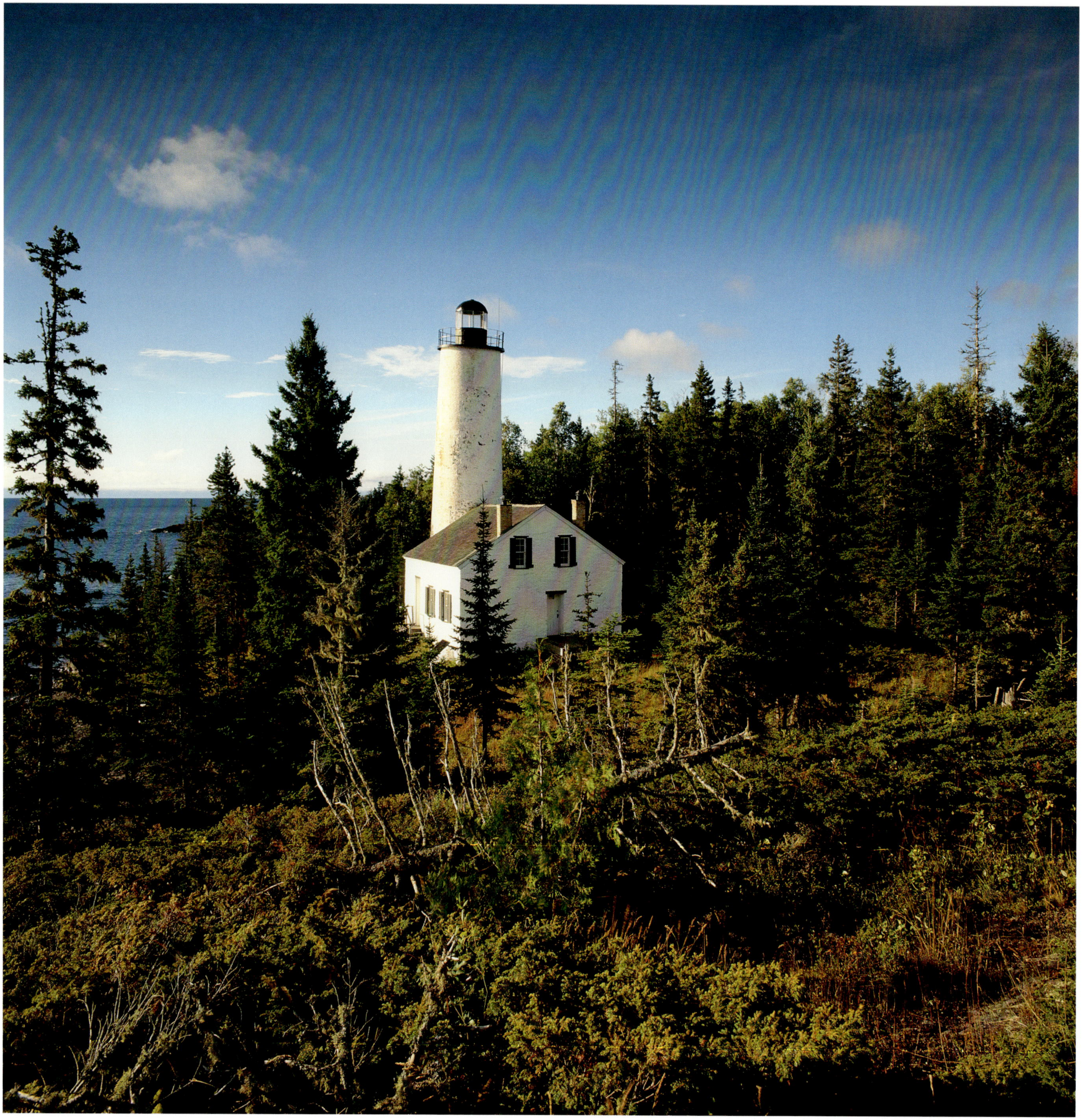

GRAND HAVEN ◄ *Est. 1839 Lake Michigan*

ROCK HARBOR, ISLE ROYALE ◄ *Est. 1855 Lake Superior*

Grand Haven ▲ Est. 1839 Lake Michigan

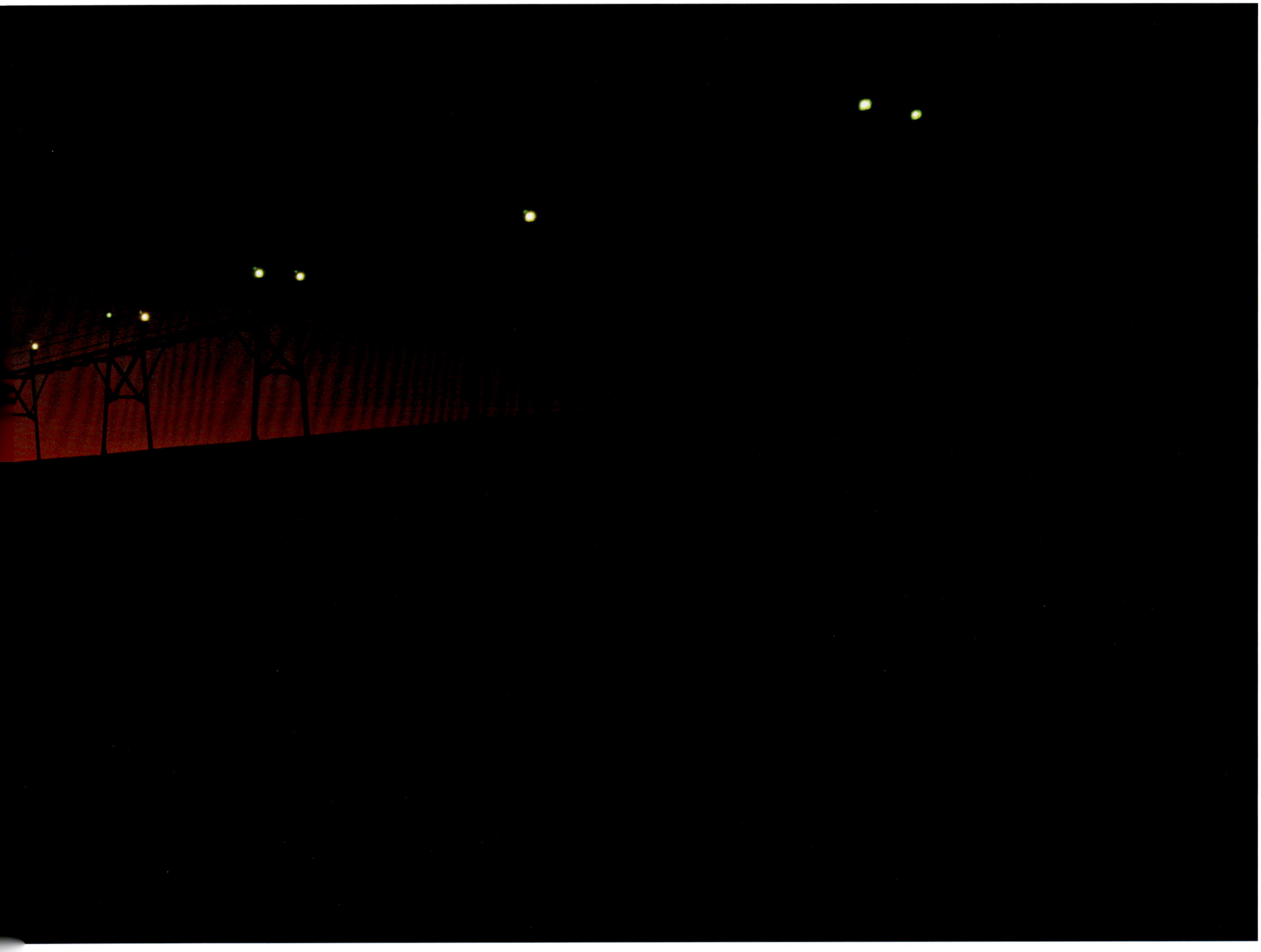

SAILING TOWARD ST. HELENA ISLAND   *Straits of Mackinac, Lake Michigan*

MARQUETTE HARBOR LIGHT △ *Est. 1853 Lake Superior*

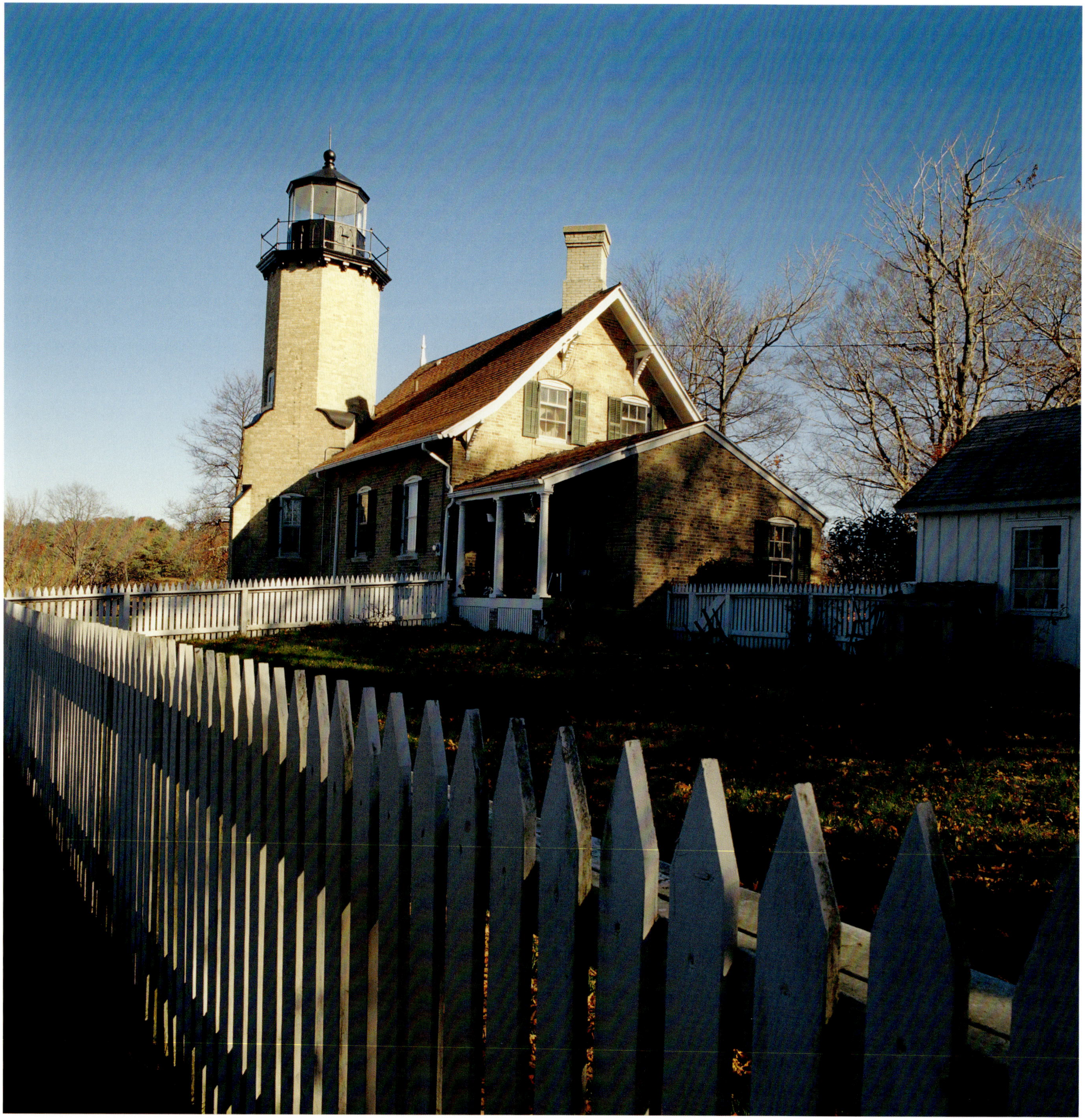

ST. HELENA ISLAND ◭   *Est. 1873 Lake Michigan*

WHITE RIVER ◀   *Est. 1875 Lake Michigan*

Liquid Shoreline   Thunder Bay Island Preserve, Lake Huron

Rock Harbor, Isle Royale ▲ *Est. 1855 Lake Superior*

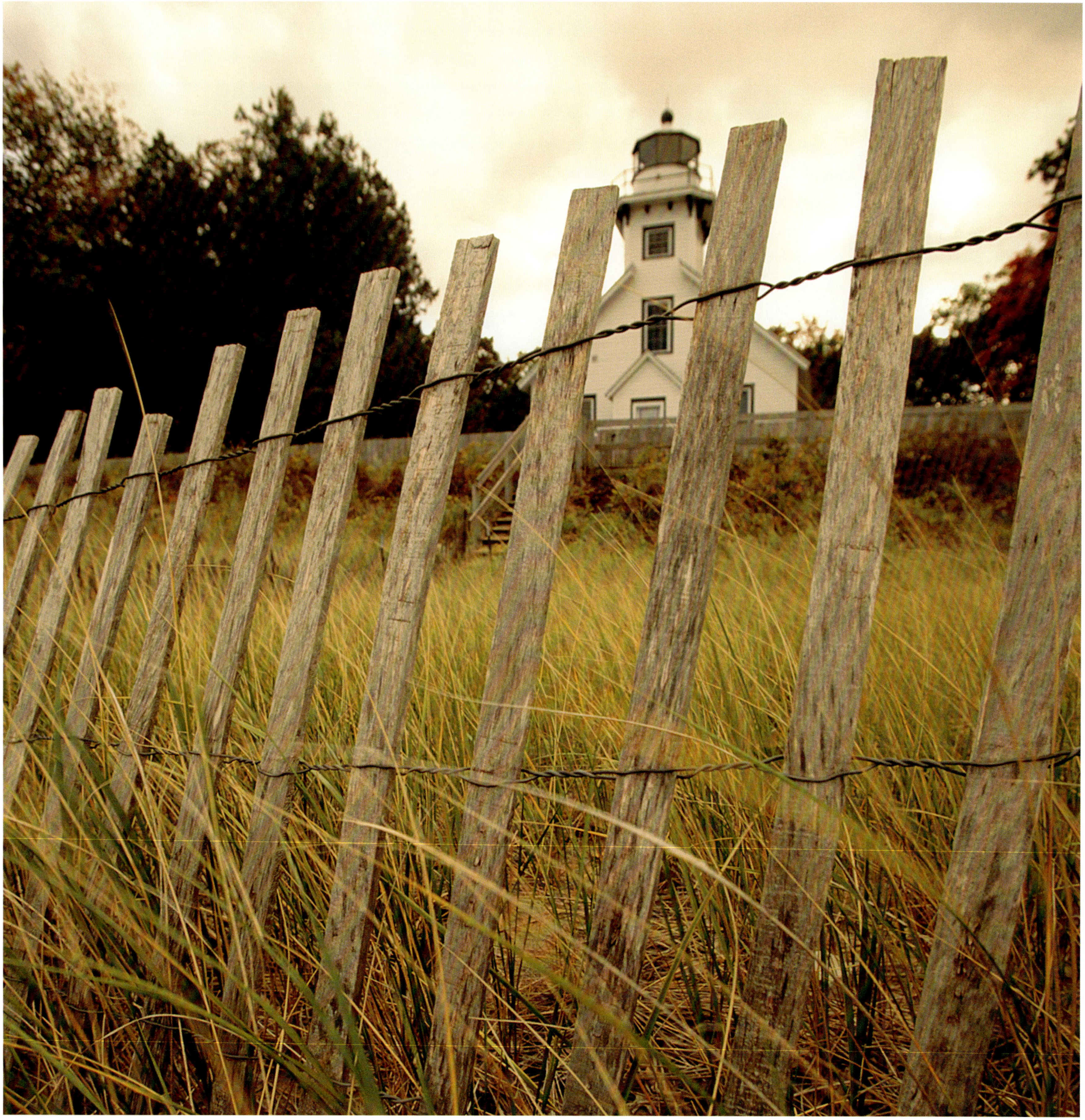

FORT GRATIOT ▲ *Est. 1825 Lake Huron*

OLD MISSION ◄ *Est. 1870 Lake Michigan*

FRANKFORT NORTH BREAKWATER ▲ *Est. 1873 Lake Michigan*

Tawas Point ⚓ Est. 1853 Lake Michigan

POINT IROQUOIS ▲ *Est. 1855 Lake Superior*

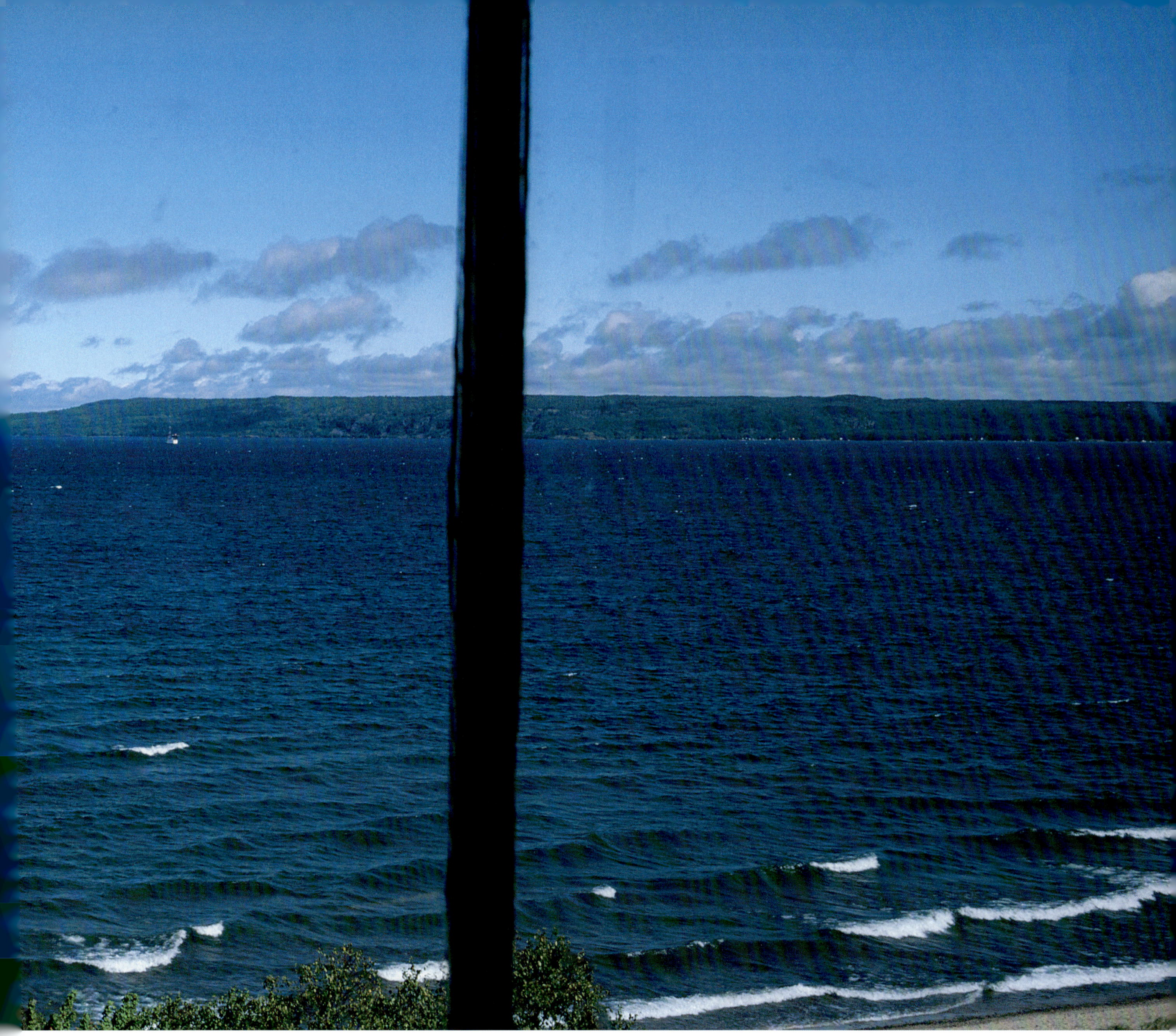

SHIPWRECK *JOSEPH S. FAY* △ *Forty Mile Point, Lake Huron*
SHIPWRECK REMAINS POUNDED BY WAVES ▷ *Pictured Rocks National Lakeshore*

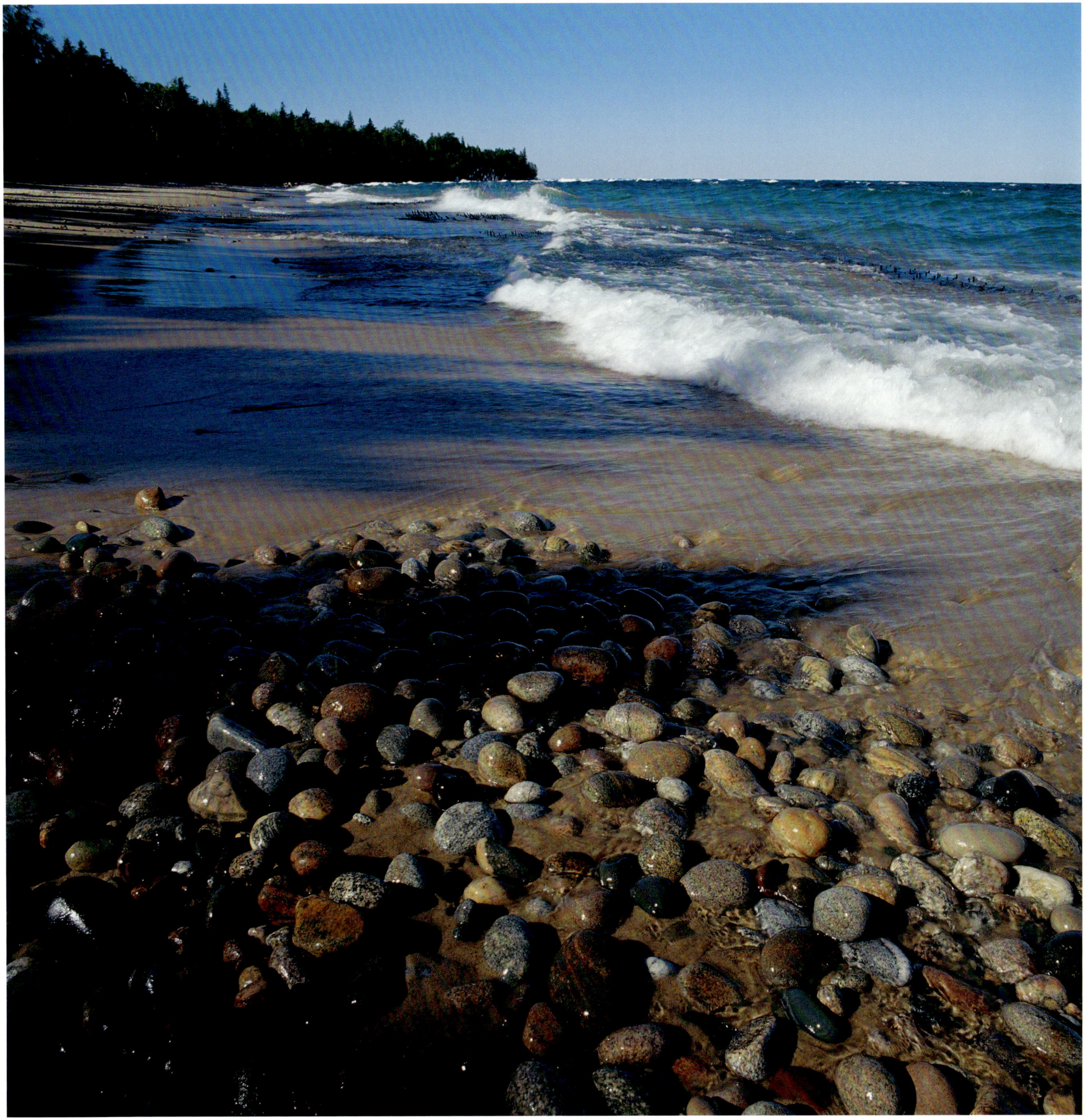

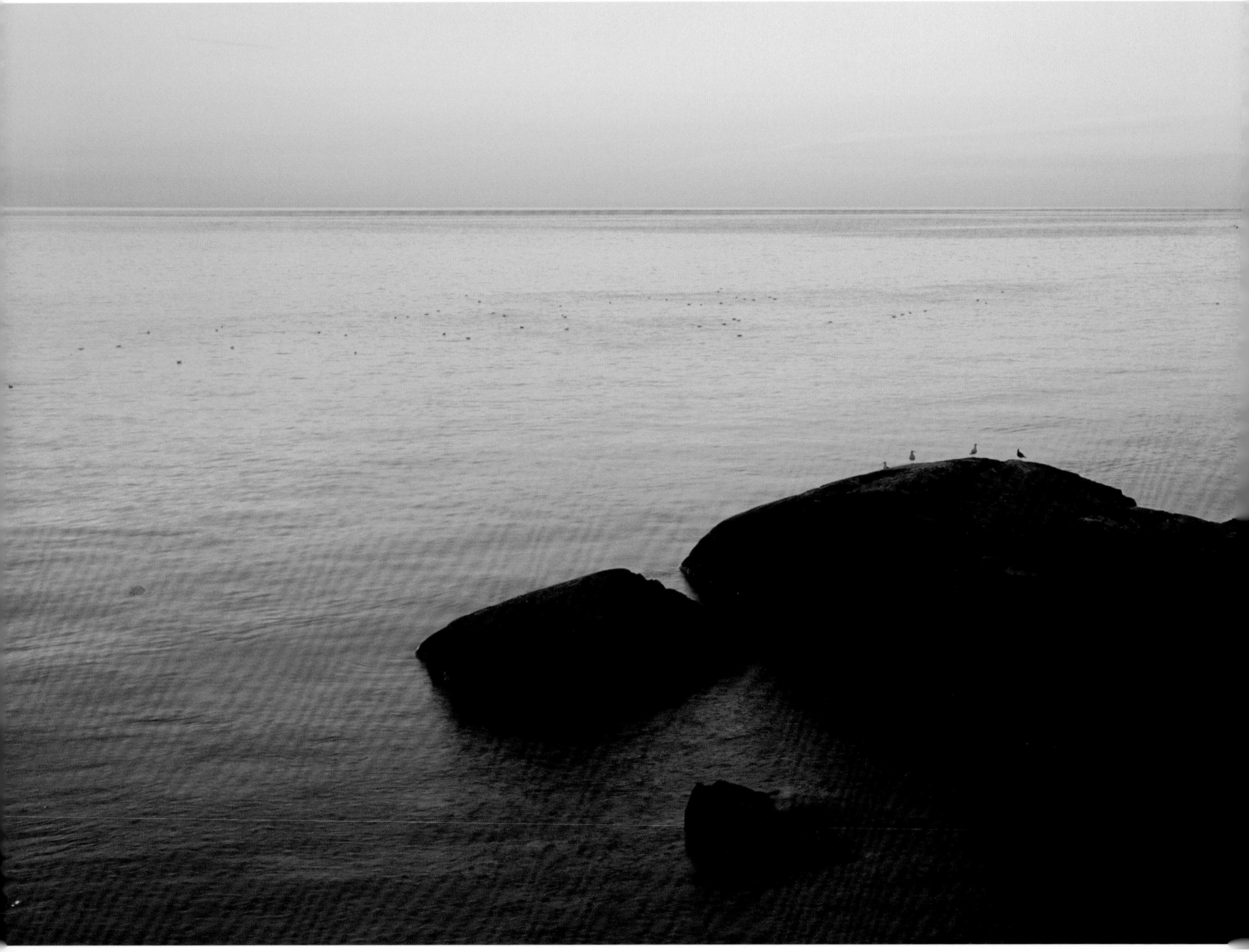

HERRING GULLS ALONG SHORELINE △ *Granite Island, Lake Superior*

PATH TO WATER'S EDGE ▲ *Tawas Point State Park, Lake Huron*

Flowers Bloom Amidst the Rocks   ▲   *Thunder Bay Island, Lake Huron*

SEUL CHOIX POINTE   ▲   *Est. 1892 Lake Michigan*

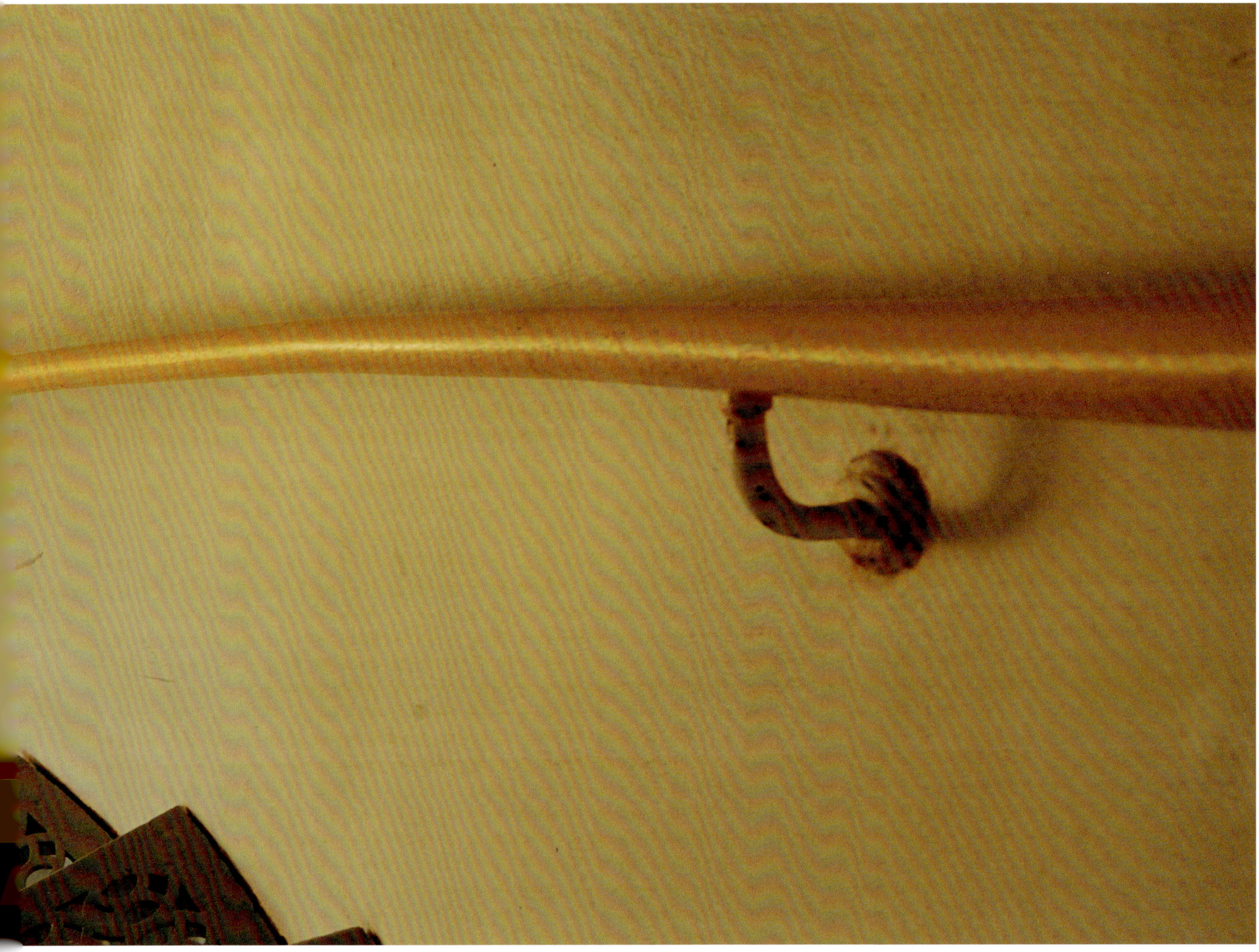

BURIAL SITE NEAR ROCK HARBOR △ *Isle Royale National Park*

ST. HELENA ISLAND ▷ *Est. 1873 Lake Michigan*

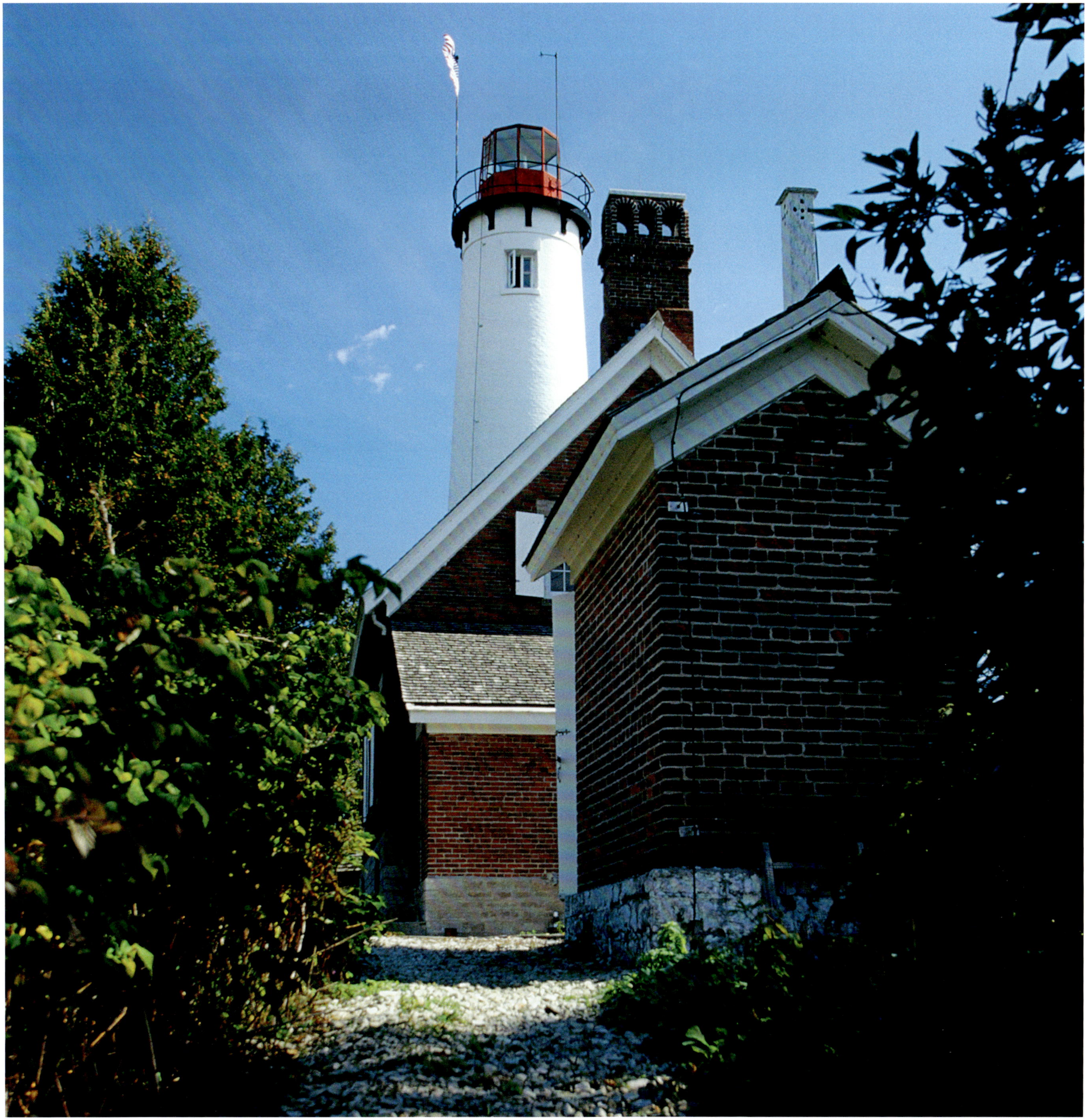

Rock Harbor, Isle Royale   △   Est. 1855 Lake Superior

GRANITE ISLAND ▲ *Est. 1868 Lake Superior*

MARQUETTE HARBOR LIGHT ▲ *Est. 1853 Lake Superior*

Old Mackinac Point ▲ Est. 1890 Lake Huron

Shells Lace the Beach *Seul Choix Pointe, Lake Michigan*

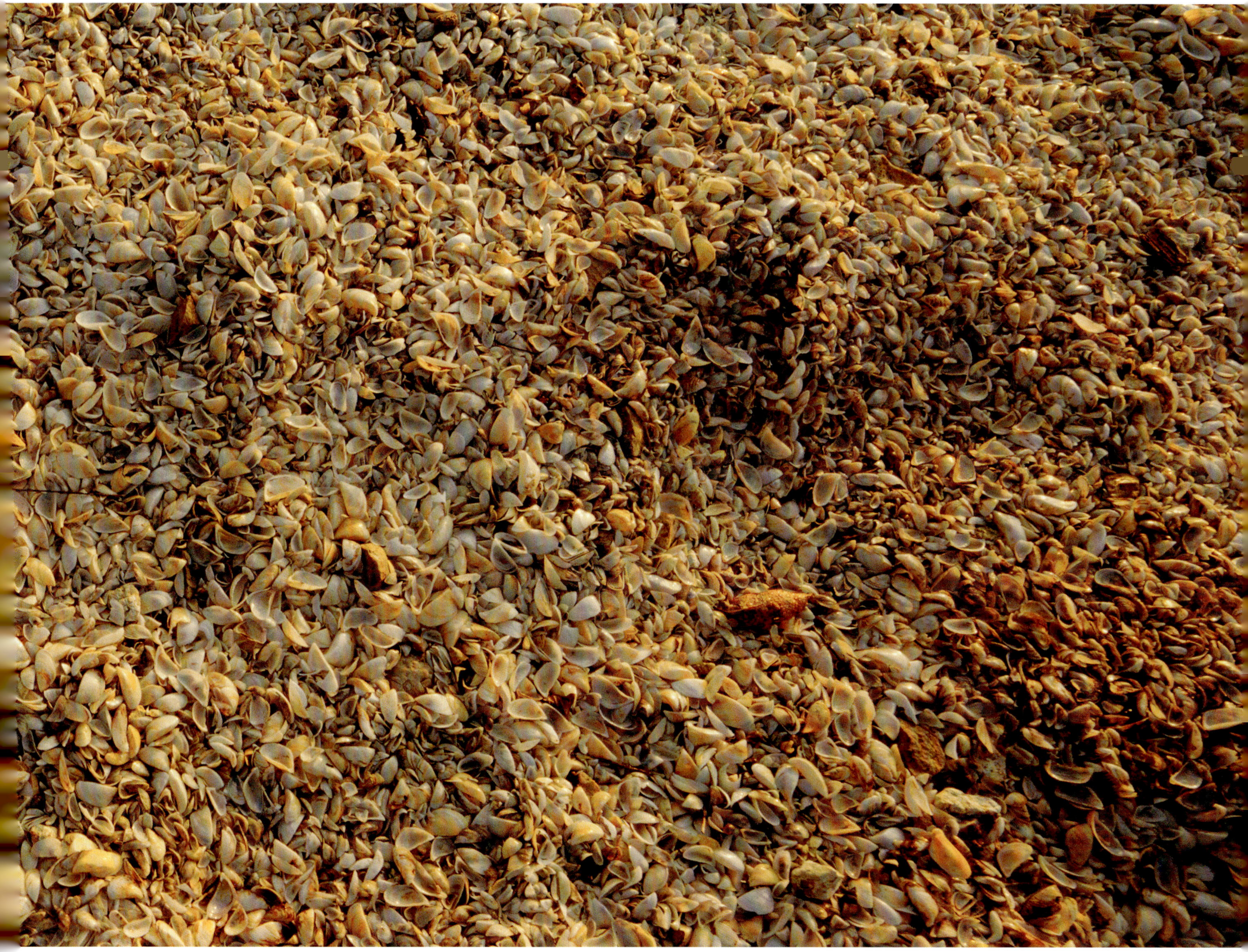

South Manitou Island ▲ Est. 1839 Lake Michigan

FORTY MILE POINT ▲ *Est. 1897 Lake Huron*

Shipwreck Remains on Beachhead ▲ *Pictured Rocks National Lakeshore*

ZIGZAG PIER AT SUNSET ▲ *Point Betsie, Lake Michigan*

ST. HELENA ISLAND ▲ *Est. 1873 Lake Michigan*

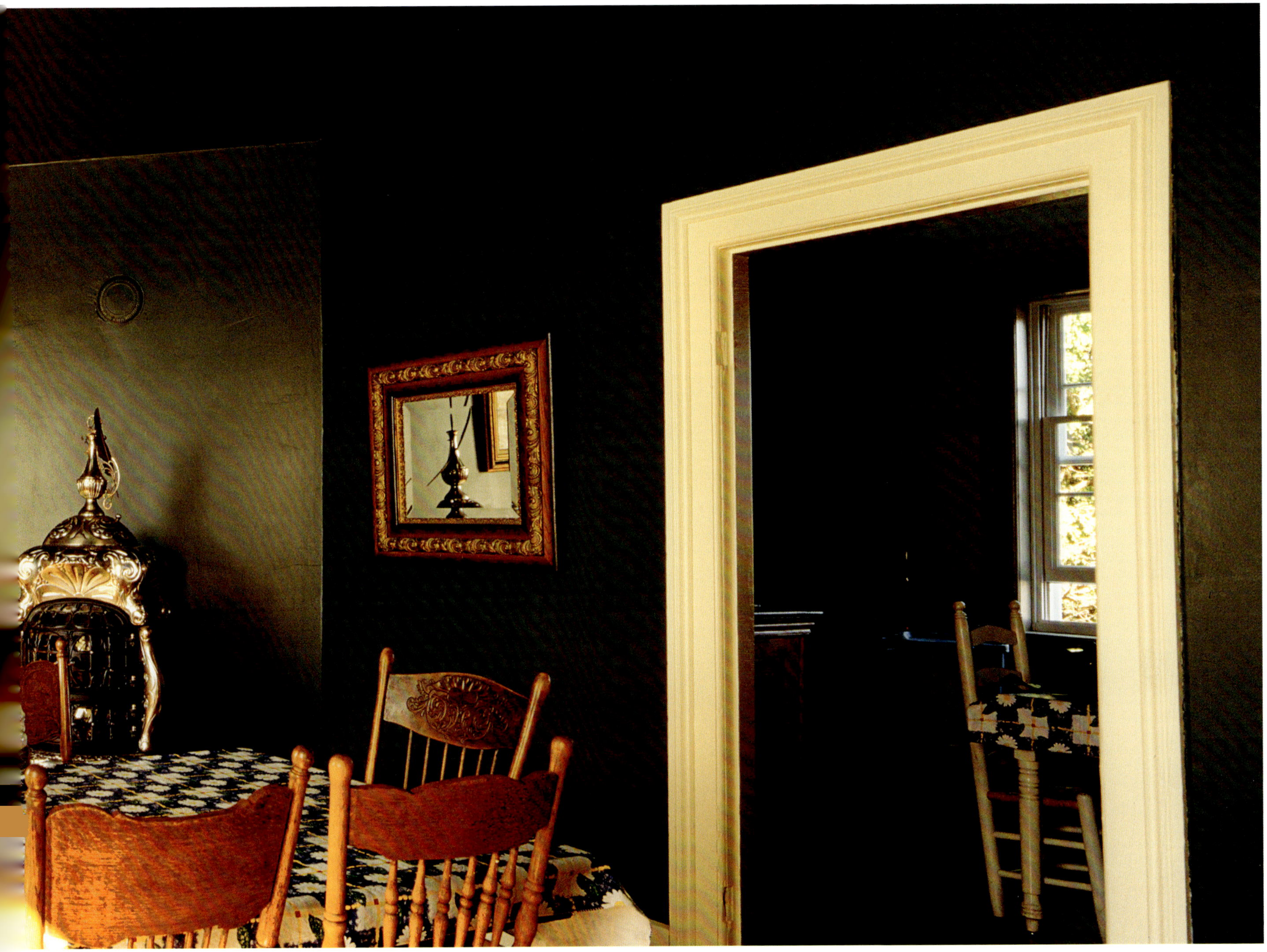

EAGLE HARBOR ▲ *Est. 1851 Lake Superior*

SHIPWRECK REMAINS ⚓ *Thunder Bay Island, Lake Huron*

COPPER HARBOR ▲   *Est. 1849 Lake Superior*
AU SABLE POINT ▶   *Est. 1874 Lake Superior*

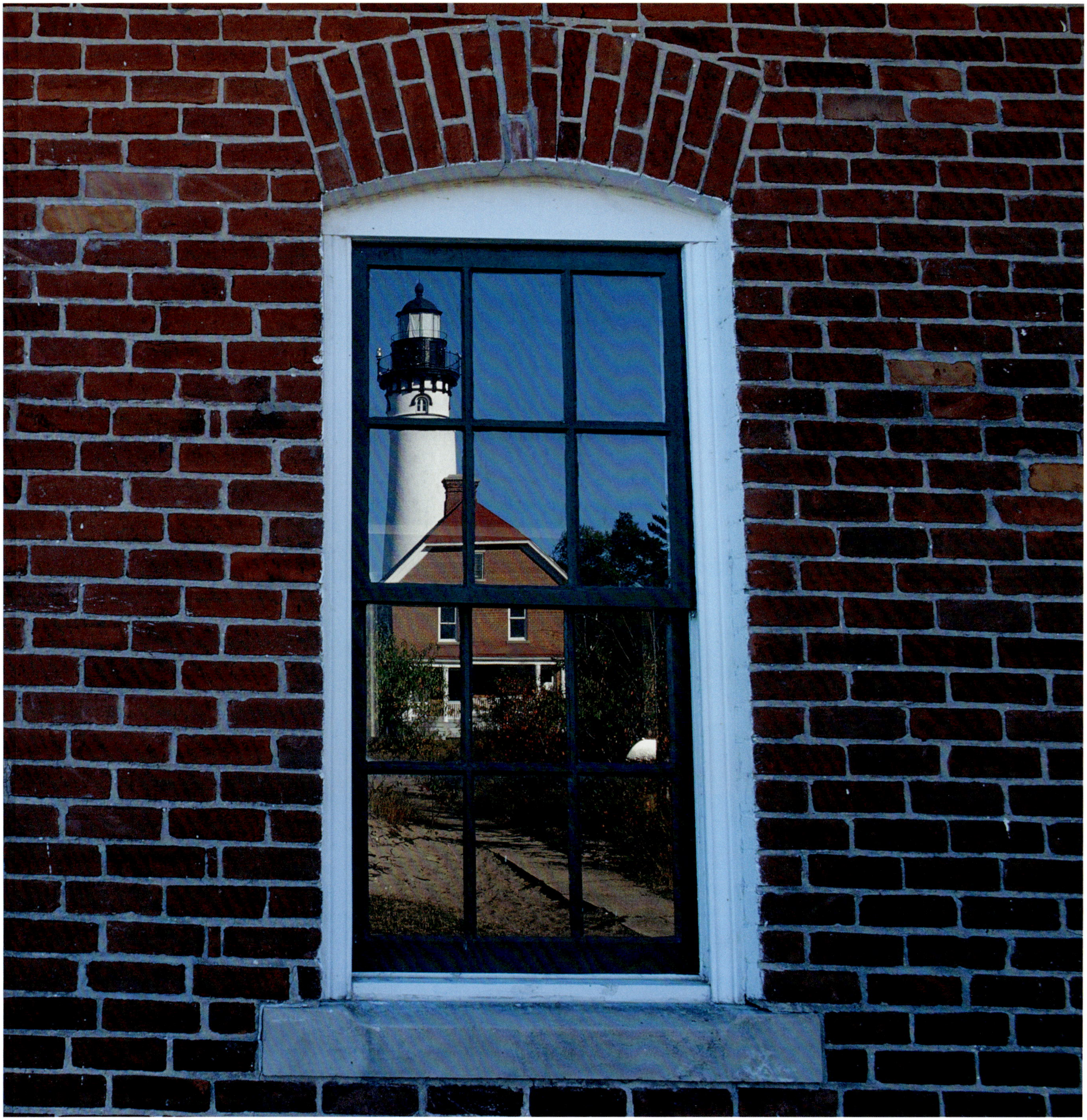

WHITE RIVER   *Est. 1875 Lake Michigan*

THUNDER BAY ISLAND ▲ *Est. 1832 Lake Huron*

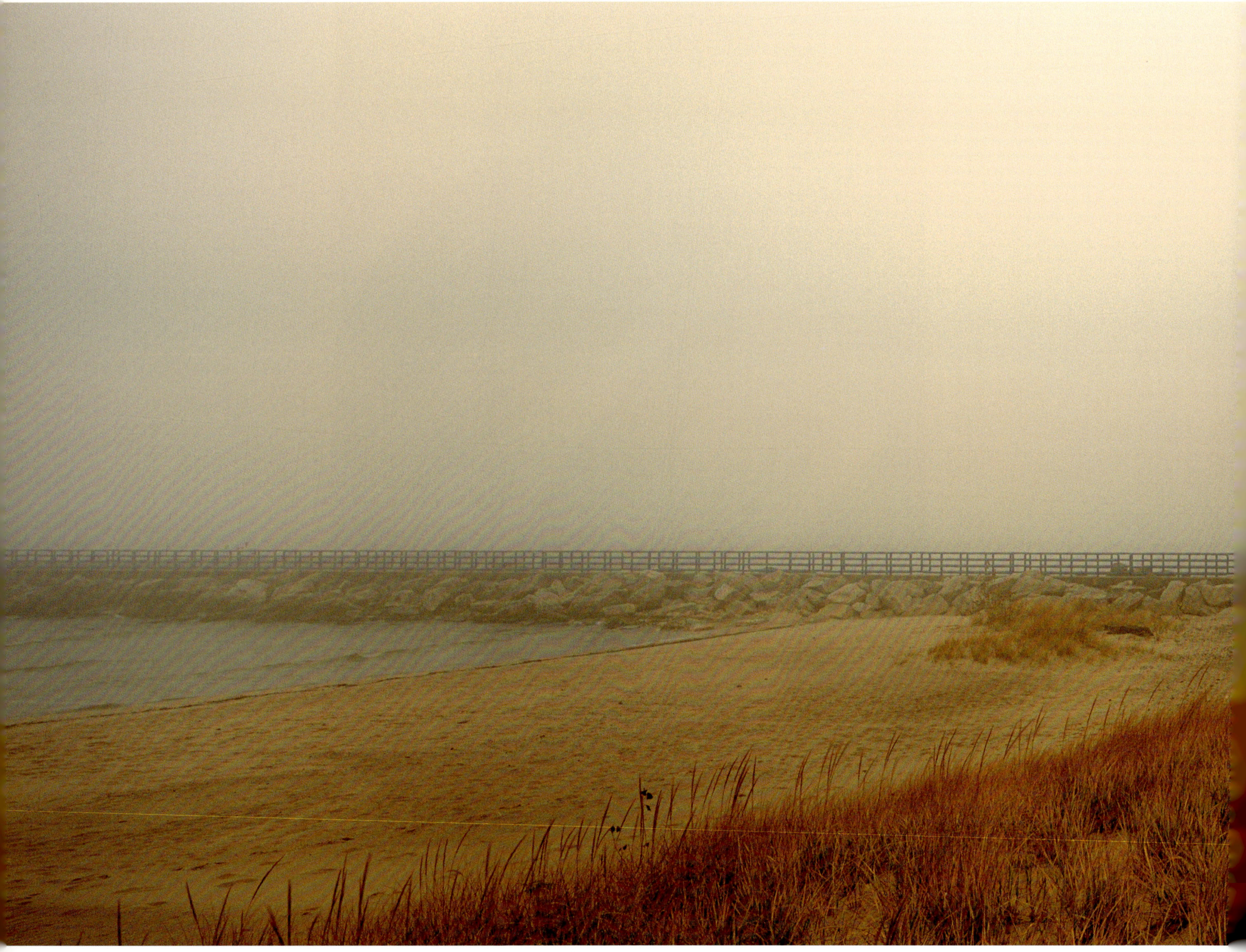

HOLLAND ▲ *Est. 1872 Lake Michigan*

ST. HELENA ISLAND △ *Est. 1873 Lake Michigan*

Whitefish Point ⚓ *Est. 1848 Lake Superior*

GRANITE ISLAND ▲ *Est. 1868 Lake Superior*

ST. JOSEPH NORTH PIER ▲ *Est. 1832 Lake Michigan*

GRANITE ISLAND △ *Est. 1868 Lake Superior*

Big Bay Point Est. 1896 Lake Superior

Little Sable Point   ▲   *Est. 1874 Lake Michigan*

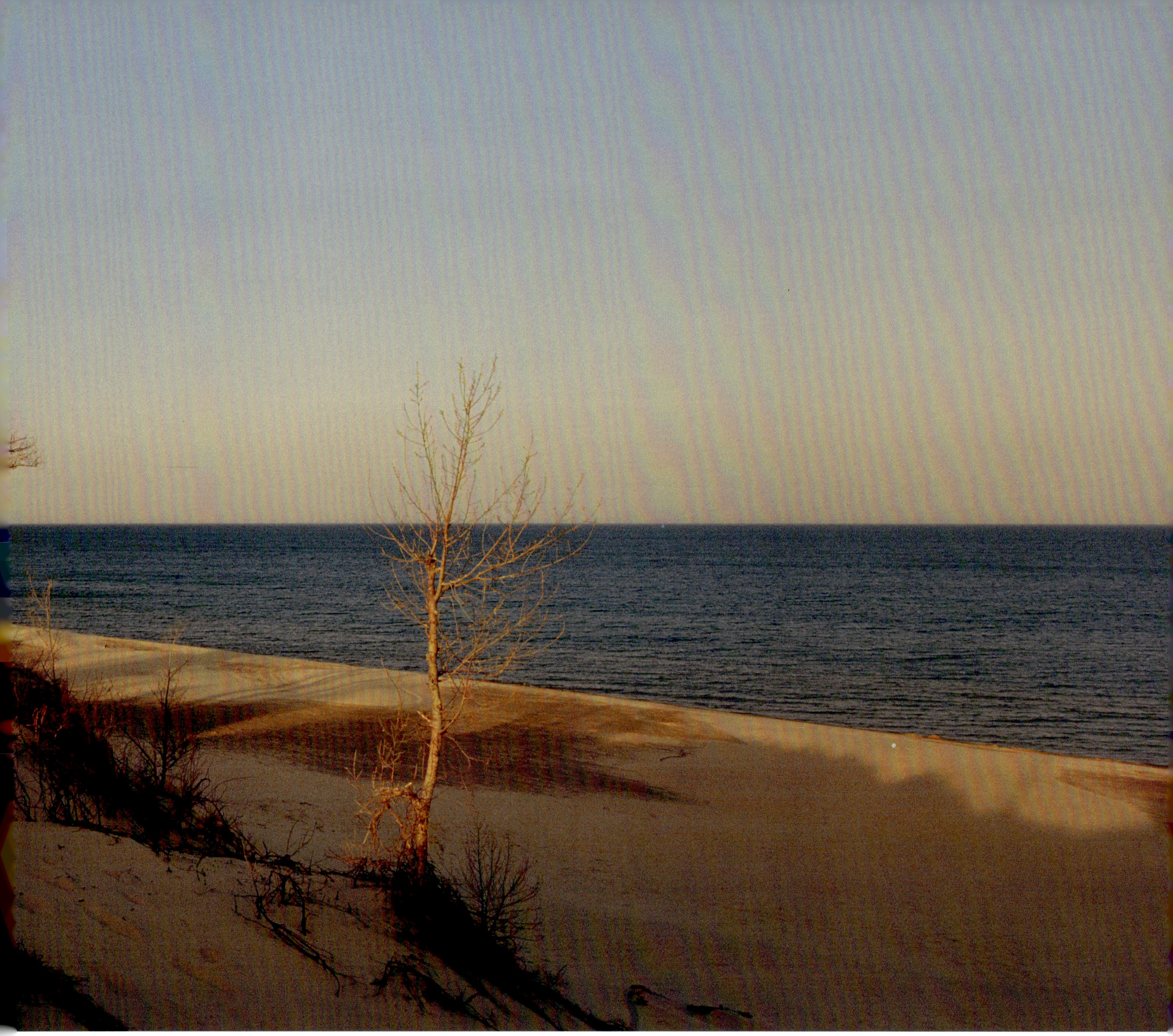

PORT SANILAC ▲ *Est. 1886 Lake Huron*

HOLLAND ▲ Est. 1872 Lake Michigan

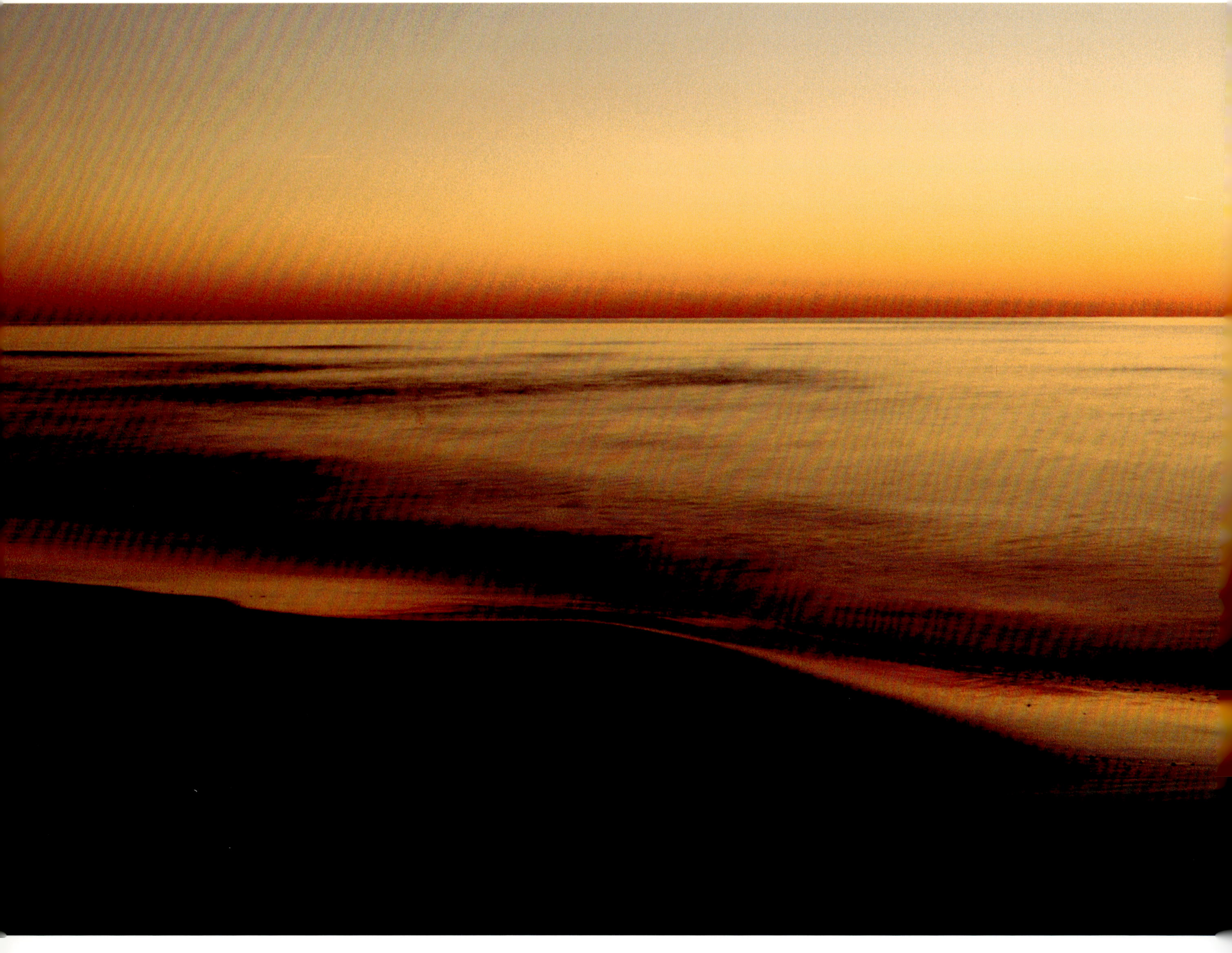

GRAND HAVEN ▲ *Est. 1839 Lake Michigan*

Afterword

THE FOLLOWING ESSAYS WERE WRITTEN BY a few of the many enthusiastic, dedicated, hard-working individuals and organizations that help preserve Michigan's lighthouse heritage. Throughout Michigan are many other wonderful, extraordinary groups that are helping tackle the preservation efforts needed to keep this heritage alive and well. So please, the next time you are wondering where you should spend your next free weekend, consider visiting and exploring one of the many wonderful lighthouses of Michigan.

Thunder Bay Island Lighthouse
Susan Skibbe
A Brief Overview from a Preservationist's Heart

Different people have different things that trigger their motivation; for a true preservationist it is much the same. Those involved with the restoration and preservation of Thunder Bay Island Light Station are equally split on why they make the eleven mile trip from shore to the island. The majority of those in our society would tell you that it is the human history that drives them to continue to do their best to insure that the island is preserved. Once one begins to delve into the history of the people before us who had such an impact on not only the island, but the local community as well, we have a moral obligation to preserve their memory. Buildings are just buildings, but when you add the human history then they become part of our legacy. That is what drives us to raise money, work hard, brave the seas, and continue to do historical research—so that the next generations will have what's left of the light station still intact and be able to understand and appreciate all that was endured and accomplished by its existence.

Restoring Granite Island Light Station
Scott L. Holman

Granite Island Light Station, located six miles off the northern shores of the Upper Peninsula of Michigan, sits atop 2½ acres of the world's oldest, glacially carved rock formations, sixty feet above the frigid, clear, and stormy waters of Lake Superior.

Built in 1868 and abandoned in 1937 as the U.S. Coast Guard took over the U.S. Lighthouse Service from the Department of Commerce and began automating its aids to navigation, Granite Island and its lighthouse became the first to be shed in a budget move in 1999.

Scott and Martine Holman were the successful bidders out of a field of 85 at a government auction. They were moved by the intrigue and adventure of owning an island and Scott's years of shipwreck exploration in Lake Superior. Living vicariously in the footsteps of the adventurous lighthouse keepers who walked the island well over a century earlier really became the drive and motivation for restoring the 131-year-old lighthouse.

While waiting for the ice to clear and the weather to permit their first visit to the island six months after their purchase, visits to the National Archives and other research prepared them for the history of the island. What they were not prepared for was the deteriorated condition of the lighthouse and the massive restoration project ahead of them. The passion developed as they dug into the richness and depth of the history of this light station and the role it played in developing industries and lives in the

Granite Island

Upper Peninsula. As they looked at the sad condition of the lighthouse, it was clear how fragile this connection with our history was.

After 2½ years of stabilizing and renovating the Granite Island Light Station, a visit to the island provides a walk into the past, transporting the new owners into the daily lives, routines, and dangers facing the early keepers—those guardians of the treacherous shipping lanes as the iron range was being built by the ancestors of Ishpeming native Scott Holman.

Looking back on their restoration and then seeing the well-intended struggle many nonprofit groups go through to volunteer their time on-site, attempting to raise the necessary money for the many lighthouses that are being shed by the Coast Guard, only to become frustrated by the lack of progress, it is clear that there is a place for private ownership. Granite Island Light Station was the first to be offered under the shedding or disposal program. Private ownership has since been deterred by a change in the law giving nonprofits the same status as a government entity.

Although the Holmans take their hats off to dedicated nonprofit volunteers, in many cases the lack of funding places our lighthouse heritage at great risk.

Nature itself would make Granite Island inaccessible to most, but the Holmans share their experience and passion. Their website displays the chronological history, the restoration process, and the final results to a worldwide public at www.graniteisland.com, beaming images from live cameras, the weather station, photos, and videos

St. Helena Island Light Station
Dick Moehl
Great Lakes Lighthouse Keepers Association

"The Miracle of the Straits of Mackinac," some have exclaimed after their working experience at the historic St. Helena Island Light Station in northern Lake Michigan, seven miles west of the Mackinac Bridge.

Today's world is left behind as you leave Mackinaw City on the workboat *Cake & Ice Cream* and travel across the Straits and back in time to the historic island and light station. There is neither electricity nor running water, and the bathroom is a privy. People wonderfully adjust to the 1800s lifestyle and find new personal inner peace and strength, as well as a rare understanding of exactly how difficult life was and how important the "community" of fellow workers used to be.

The award-winning historic restoration is nearly complete after thousands of hours of effort donated by hundreds of diligent, eager workers from Boy and Girl Scout troops, church groups, and the Great Lakes Lighthouse Keepers Association (GLLKA) members. In addition, hundreds of educators have studied and worked during the GLLKA's Maritime Heritage Educators Workshops since 1989. They in turn have imparted the knowledge and skills learned at St. Helena to tens of thousands of students all over the United States.

Perhaps the greatest value stemming from the St. Helena Island Light Station restoration is the "ownership" garnered by the workers who have experienced "The Miracle of the Straits of Mackinac" while reliving the life of the keeper at a working light station. What today's keepers "own" they protect.

We call this the "Development of a New Generation of Preservationists." We believe this process is key to a lasting and meaningful future for any historic property.

Whitefish Point Light
Tom Farnquist

Whitefish Point Light Station — established 1849
National Historic Site, owned and operated by the
Great Lakes Shipwreck Historical Society

Great Lakes' mariners have recognized Whitefish Point as Lake Superior's most important lighthouse for over 150 years. This light remains an active aid to navigation maintained by the U.S. Coast Guard. It is the oldest operating lighthouse on Lake Superior.

Its beacon continues to warn up bound vessel traffic of "Lake Superior's Shipwreck Coast"— a treacherous 80-mile shoreline that stretches westward to Munising, Michigan, infamous for having claimed Superior's greatest concentration of shipwrecks. To down bound vessels, the light signals a critical turning point that often shows mariners the way to relatively calmer waters in Whitefish Bay.

Man's structural presence at Whitefish Point began in 1849 with the construction of Lake Superior's first lighthouse. In a few short years, this first

Whitefish Point Light

60-foot stone tower proved unable to withstand powerful winds sweeping across 250 miles of open lake. It was replaced by the present "iron-pile" light tower with a two-story keeper's quarters building, both built in 1861 at the order of President Abraham Lincoln when the nation was teetering on the verge of civil war.

The Great Lakes Shipwreck Historical Society has implemented a comprehensive and very popular program of historic restoration and museum interpretation at Whitefish Point. Exhibits tell exciting and dramatic stories of the U.S. Lighthouse Service, U.S. Life-Saving Service, and U.S. Coast Guard, three governmental agencies whose common mission has always been to make travel on Lake Superior safer for mariners. Here at the Great Lakes Shipwreck Museum Complex exhibits capture the exciting legacy of shipwrecks, heroic rescues, and tragic loss of life along these shores—the most recent and famous having been 29 men aboard the steamer *Edmund Fitzgerald*, lost just 17 miles northwest of this lighthouse on November 10, 1975.

More than 75,000 visitors are drawn to Whitefish Point each year for several reasons— interests in lighthouses, shipwrecks, the Life-Saving Service, Coast Guard, local history, and the natural environment. Whitefish Point is also an important point along the North American flyway for migrating avian species. These themes combine to offer an inspiring blend of both human and natural history. The Shipwreck Museum's dedication to top-quality presentations has earned prominence for this historic site among Michigan's maritime cultural attractions.

Tourism has become the predominant industry of Michigan's Upper Peninsula. Through professionally designed, popular exhibits, the Whitefish Point Light Station/Great Lakes Shipwreck Museum Complex has had a powerful, positive effect on the area's fragile economy. The museum is open seasonally May 1 through October 31.

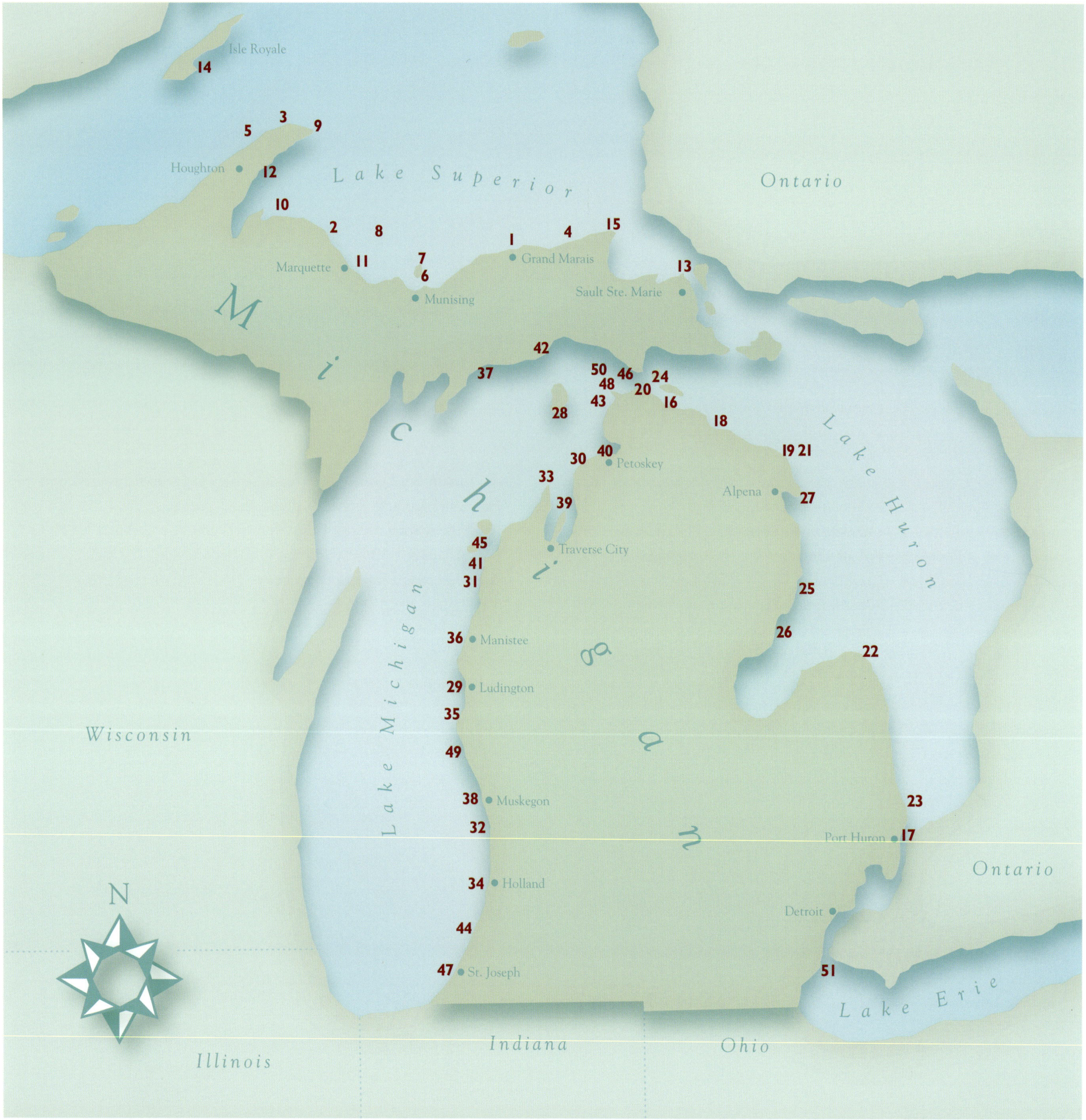

Isle Royale
14
5
3
9
Houghton
12
Lake Superior
Ontario
10
2
8
1
4
15
Marquette
11
7
6
Grand Marais
13
Munising
Sault Ste. Marie
Michigan
42
37
50
46
24
48
20
43
16
28
18
Lake Huron
30
40
Petoskey
19
21
33
Alpena
27
39
45
Traverse City
41
31
25
Lake Michigan
36
Manistee
26
22
29
Ludington
35
Wisconsin
49
38
Muskegon
23
32
Port Huron
17
Ontario
N
34
Holland
Detroit
44
47
St. Joseph
51
Lake Erie
Indiana
Ohio
Illinois

Michigan Lighthouses

(*year established and closest town*)

Lake Superior

1. Au Sable Point *Est. 1874, Grand Marais*
2. Big Bay Point *Est. 1896, Big Bay*
3. Copper Harbor *Est. 1849, Copper Harbor*
4. Crisp Point *Est. 1904, Paradise*
5. Eagle Harbor *Est. 1851, Eagle Harbor*
6. Grand Island East Channel *Est. 1868, Munising*
7. Grand Island Old North *Est. 1855, Munising*
8. Granite Island *Est. 1868, Marquette*
9. Gull Rock *Est. 1867, Copper Harbor*
10. Huron Island *Est. 1868, Skanee*
11. Marquette Harbor Light *Est. 1853, Marquette*
12. Mendota (Bete Grise) *Est. 1870, Mendota*
13. Point Iroquois *Est. 1855, Brimley*
14. Rock Harbor *Est. 1855, Isle Royale*
15. Whitefish Point *Est. 1849, Paradise*

Lake Huron

16. Cheyboygan Crib Light *Est. 1884, Cheyboygan*
17. Fort Gratiot *Est. 1825, Port Huron*
18. Forty Mile Point *Est. 1897, Rogers City*
19. New Presque Isle *Est. 1870, Presque Isle*
20. Old Mackinac Point *Est. 1890, Mackinaw City*
21. Old Presque Isle *Est. 1840, Presque Isle*
22. Pointe Aux Barque *Est. 1848, Port Austin*
23. Port Sanilac *Est. 1886, Port Sanilac*
24. Round Island *Est. 1896, Mackinac Island*
25. Sturgeon Point *Est. 1870, Harrisville*
26. Tawas Point *Est. 1853, Tawas*
27. Thunder Bay Island *Est. 1832, Alpena*

Lake Michigan

28. Beaver Island *Est. 1852, St. James*
29. Big Sable Point *Est. 1867, Ludington*
30. Charlevoix South Pierhead *Est. 1914, Charlevoix*
31. Frankfort North Breakwater *Est. 1873, Frankfort*
32. Grand Haven *Est. 1839, Grand Haven*
33. Grand Traverse *Est. 1853, Northport*
34. Holland *Est. 1872, Holland*
35. Little Sable Point *Est. 1874, Mears*
36. Manistee North Pierhead *Est. 1875, Manistee*
37. Manistique East Breakwater *Est. 1915, Manistique*
38. Muskegon South Pierhead *Est. 1851, Muskegon*
39. Old Mission *Est. 1870, Traverse City*
40. Petoskey Pierhead *Est. 1899, Petoskey*
41. Point Betsie *Est. 1858, Frankfort*
42. Seul Choix Pointe *Est. 1895, Gulliver*
43. Skillagalee (Ile Aux Galets) *Est. 1850, Cross Village*
44. South Haven *Est. 1872, South Haven*
45. South Manitou Island *Est. 1839, Leland*
46. St. Helena Island *Est. 1873, St. Ignace*
47. St. Joseph North Pier *Est. 1832, St. Joseph*
48. Waugoshance *Est. 1832, Mackinaw City*
49. White River *Est. 1875, Whitehall*
50. White Shoal *Est. 1910, Mackinaw City*

Lake Erie

51. Detroit River *Est. 1885, Detroit*

Holland Lighthouse

Acknowledgments

This project would not have been possible without the generous help and support of the following individuals and businesses: Boat captain Karl Gretzinger and his co-captain Ben; to my friends at See North; pilot Greg Putalik; Isle Royale Air Service; boat captain Troy Wood and crew; Pat Guddall at Westphoto; Mike Lussier at AGX Imaging; Mike DiCosola at Chromaticity; Kevin Carlini at Woolrich; Leanne Franzman at Lowepro; pilot Luther Kurtz and company; Tom Farnquist, Executive Director of the Great Lakes Shipwreck Society; Petoskey Central Elementary School teacher Mrs. Jean Dell; Cake and Ice Cream boat captain Sandy Planisek; Mr. Dick Moehl, President of the Great Lakes Lighthouse Keepers Association; Cherry Capital Aviation and pilot Wayne Braden; Mr. and Mrs. Scott Holman; Susan Skibbe; Stephan Tongue; Bill and Mary Ann Donahue; Barb and Bill Weideman; Chris West; Jim and Carol Kelly; Jim; Skip; Lynne; and Carol; and to all of the wonderfully supportive lighthouse enthusiasts whom I met along the way! *Thank you all so very much!*

Sponsors

Woolrich *for providing outdoor clothing*
www.woolrich.com

WOOLRICH EST. 1830
The Original Outdoor Clothing Company®

AgxImaging *for providing the finest E-6 Film Processing available*
1-906-632-1850

AgX

Chromaticity, Inc. *for providing Color Management*
1642 Broadway NW, Suite 100
Grand Rapids, MI 49504
1-616-361-7773
www.chromaticity.com

CHROMATICITY INCORPORATED

Lowepro *for providing Photo Backpack (Dryzone Bags)*
1-800-800-5693
www.lowepro.com

Lowepro